# Gratitude Through Hard Times

## Finding Positive Benefits Through Our Darkest Hours

### Chris Schembra

First edition published June 2022

Book interior design: Jess LaGreca, Mayfly Design
Illustrations: Sonia Corredor
Research Coordinator: Madeline Haslam
Question Designer: Court Roberts

ISBN (hardback) 9798986212319
ISBN (paperback) 9798986212302
ISBN (ebook) 9798986212326

www.747club.org

*Dedicated to
Andrew Schembra and Scott Stibitz*

# Table of Contents

# A Brief Introduction to Gratitude

*"The deep craving of human nature
is the need to be appreciated."*
– William James

# My Humble Gratitude Beginnings

*"I discovered that a fresh start is a process.*
*A fresh start is a journey—a journey that requires a plan."*
– Vivian Jokotade

My personal gratitude journey began when I returned from a trip to Rome in 2015. At the time, I was involved in the theater industry, running a production company alongside the Emmy Award-winning, Tony-nominated actor Tony Lo Bianco. He, his wife Alyse, and I had been living the high life, traveling around to charity galas and various countries, using theater as a tool for learning and connection.

We had worked on several incredibly interesting projects, garnered the respect of our peers, received some accolades, and even made some money along the way. My childhood friends and family were calling me on a weekly basis to congratulate me on finding a solid career path, working and living in the Big Apple, and involving myself with some people and projects they recognized. But as good as my life looked good on paper, I felt the polar opposite: broken on the inside.

The more people mentioned my success, the more I felt like a fraud.

My general sense of malaise was thick by July of 2015. Tony, Alyse, and I had just returned home to New York City after producing a Broadway play in Italy, and I felt lonely, unfulfilled, disconnected, and insecure in my tiny studio apartment on the Upper West Side of Manhattan. I was overwhelmed, anxious as hell, and unable to see a clearing through the forest.

I imagine many of you are feeling that way right now.

Why was I so down? Well, Rome had changed my entire perspective and opened me up to the possibilities of what life could be. It was inspiring to soak in *La Dolce Vita* (the good life), and see how the Romans walked, dressed, and honored their robust history.

I'd stayed up late talking to new friends until the wee hours of the morning. I'd navigated the walkways of Trastevere; basked in perfect sunsets on Ponte Umberto; dined at Da Enzo, Il Bacaro, and Caffe Sant Eustachio. I'd become addicted to the way Italians lived life. They weren't consumed by what material possessions they could acquire, and instead valued rest, reflection, and creating genuine connection amongst their communities. They knew how to *tranquille, piano*—to slow down and just relax.

I hadn't enjoyed such a pace since I was a kid, running barefoot along beaches and shrimping through the salt marshes on tiny Hilton Head Island. Though I had grown up slowly in sunny South Carolina, I'd since gotten sucked up into the fast-paced life of New York City. And though my life may have seemed glamorous to the outside world, I felt like I'd been chewed up and spit out.

I knew I had to change the way I was feeling, and slow down *pronto*; otherwise I was going to be swallowed up by my despair. The last time I'd felt so empty was in my early twenties, when

I went down a deep, dark path of depression, self-injury, jail, and rehab . . .

Suffice to say, I didn't want to go back.

So, I thought, *What was it about Rome that had felt so good?* Well, it was the food. More specifically, it was how the Romans ate their food—in community, with family and friends new and old. It was how they created a sense of belonging, and did so authentically.

I thought I could begin there, working to re-create the connection I felt in Italy by sharing good meals and thoughtful conversation with friends. It started with a simple pot of pasta sauce and fifteen friends coming over to cook, serve each other, and have a good meal.

My first dinner in my New York studio—only 300 square feet—was a far cry from the splendid tables of Rome, the Eternal City. But I learned that the secret sauce wasn't designing a beautiful tablescape, or even serving the freshest ingredients. It was creating a space to share stories on a subject that's both universal and intimate: the people who have made an impact on our lives.

At that very first dinner, I posed a simple question: **If you could give credit or thanks to one person in your life, someone you don't thank enough, who would that be?**

That question made my guests come alive. They shared stories of people in their past who had directly or indirectly helped them get to where they were. Some of them described individuals who had shown them great generosity, unflinching loyalty, and unconditional love. They reflected on how those positive interactions shaped them into the people they had become.

Others told stories of people who had been unbelievably cruel—people who had made them feel left out, lonely, or unwanted. They had been hurt—and badly so—but in sharing around the table, they were finding the benefits in what they had endured and making it part of their story of hope and resilience. There wasn't a dry eye in the house.

After the dinner, all of the attendees kept the conversation going through email, and we decided to turn that dinner into a series of dinners. I sent out my next invitation, this time with a new rule: The first time you come, you come alone. The second time you come, you can bring a friend. After that, you are eligible to nominate someone to attend in your stead.

The size and frequency of my dinners increased quite rapidly, with people flying in from all over the world to attend. My network grew along with them, and eventually Fortune 500 CEOs, Academy Award winners, Grammy Award-winning recording artists, Super Bowl champions, Hall of Fame athletes, were among the regular attendees.

Ultimately, I quit my job in theater to produce these experiences full time. Once companies started hearing about our ability to create safe spaces, my phone really started ringing. Microsoft, Google, IBM, Dell, Salesforce, Verizon, Citi, Lyft, Ferrari, the United States Navy, Harvard, and hundreds of others invited my team and me into their organizations to produce these experiences for their teams, clients, boards of directors, channel partners, and more. Whether through small dinners, large conferences, or year-long campaigns, my team and I brought together tens of thousands of people to recognize, celebrate, and connect over the principles of gratitude.

Life was starting to make complete sense, it looked like I was finally hitting my stride. And then one day, the COVID pandemic hit.

I'd just been in Italy in February of 2020 with my father. Upon returning home to New York City, I immediately went into a 2-week quarantine, where I had to deal with the ways the world had changed—and their impact on my business—virtually overnight.

My team and I were just about to release our first book, *Gratitude and Pasta: The Secret Sauce for Human Connection*, which Forbes had ranked as 2020's number-two book to create human connection. But, thanks to the pandemic, a book about producing in-person experiences became obsolete.

What were we to do?

Our book tour was canceled, our revenue went to zero, and we even had to let a few people go.

At that moment, in March of 2020, I felt the same way I had after returning home from Italy in 2015. This time, it was COVID that had ripped the dinner table and pasta sauce away from me. For the second time in six years, I felt lonely, nervous, tired, anxious, and overwhelmed.

It sucked.

But I quickly realized I was not alone. In fact, I was surrounded by people—locally and globally—who were going through some of the toughest days of their lives.

Even in the midst of a global pandemic, their daily struggles raged on. Their husbands cheated. Their dogs died. They lost market share to the competition. Someone disappointed them.

Then, of course, there were the ways in which the pandemic made the already difficult stuff harder. Mothers were juggling working from home, home school, and everything else. Healthcare workers were camping out in hotels, attempting to partner and parent from afar while they worked on the front lines. Hospitality professionals tried to make ends meet and care for their families as work dried up, while grocery store cashiers and meal delivery drivers struggled to keep up with the demand for their services alongside their other responsibilities.

All the while, people were dying, and their loved ones couldn't be by their bedside. We couldn't hug family members or gather with friends. At times, the isolation felt unbearable. Substance abuse and suicidal ideation increased among young adults, front-line workers, and unpaid caregivers. Everyone was going through it, feeling grief, sadness, loss, fear, and anxiety.

And instead of coming together, many of us got caught up in our differences—which led to a spike in social conflict. Hatred and divisiveness rose to new heights, and we entered into a period marked by judgment, resentment, jealousy, entitlement, and unabashed greed.

Meanwhile, on the work front, people kept asking me what my team and I were going to do. Could we create something that could help break this cycle, that could help people overcome the challenges they were facing? Could we help cultivate a genuine sense of belonging when they needed it most?

After a lot of thought, we came up with a potential answer: video conferencing. What if we could pivot and start producing our experiences virtually, helping people connect authentically, resolve conflict, and feel a little less lonely when they were forced to be apart?

Six days after New York City went into lockdown, we hosted our first Virtual Gratitude Experience™ for friends and family. Our idea was off to a rough start, with eight of us coming together to talk about what we'd gone through in the past week. Everyone appreciated the opportunity to come into the present moment, hear stories from quarantine, and briefly escape what had quickly become a monotonous existence. But it just wasn't the kind of connection we'd come to know and love.

It felt more like a happy hour, rather than an intentional moment. I took a look at the model I'd built and realized we were missing one thing: gratitude.

We started asking our Signature Gratitude Question at the very next experience, and once again, the people came alive. Just like they did in person, folks were arriving into our Zoom rooms with the most amazing stories.

Attendees stepped into our experiences feeling anxious, nervous, overwhelmed, lonely, grieving, stressed, angry, and tired, but they left feeling grateful, connected, inspired, happy and joyful.

For the first time in months, they told us, they felt authentically seen and heard. And even though these experiences weren't in person, they actually reported the same feelings they got from a warm, genuine hug.

Those experiences continued every single night for free for the next few months, giving people the space to come and connect in authentic ways. Once again, companies began calling us. At a time when so many were turning to lackluster virtual wine tastings, comedy shows, webinars, and happy hours for connection, our experiences were in a league of their own. We had created a product that companies couldn't afford NOT to purchase.

We soon realized our impact from a data perspective as well. We had actually created an evidence-based framework that could guarantee a deep, meaningful, positive transformation through a ninety-minute virtual experience. In fact, after tallying the data from tens of thousands of attendees, we found our experiences had a 99.998% success rate, essentially guaranteeing a positive emotional transformation.

And with that, our fortunes had reversed. The canceled book tour, the lost revenue, and the skeleton staff was now a thing of our past. Now, instead of taking days to produce an event, we could host one in just ninety minutes over Zoom. Instead of companies having to spend hundreds of thousands of dollars flying in employees for an offsite, all they had to do was encourage them to turn on their computer screens and cameras. We were able to host our experiences multiple times per day, across different time zones, with groups of all sizes.

The more experiences we produced, the better we became at listening to the ways people needed gratitude as a means of getting through hard times. Pretty soon, we were producing all kinds of gratitude experiences online. The emails, texts, and phone calls from people sharing that our experiences had changed their entire outlook, or even saved their lives, were coming in by the dozens. We were drunk on the impact we were having with just a screen, a camera, and a virtual meeting room.

We had a good routine: David as experience coordinator, Madeline as research coordinator, Jennifer as team mom, and Sonia making us look pretty. Madeline kept feeding us insights on the science and psychology of gratitude, so we were able to explain the concrete benefits people were experiencing, and how gratitude was actually changing their brains. With seamless execution, reams of data, and thousands of inspired attendees, we convinced ourselves that we couldn't afford to stop bringing people the experiences that would change their lives.

It was more experiences, more impact, more money, more everything! Momentum was at an all-time high. There could be no end in sight. We were back, better, and bigger than ever!

And then I almost threw it all away.

Content Warning: What happened next could have ended my life. And to preface this story, I am writing this book from a good headspace and have learned a tremendous amount through the experience. I have even given gratitude to it (more on that to come).

On December 30th, 2021, I engaged with a gnarly episode of Non-Suicidal Self Injury (NSSI). NSSI refers to the intentional destruction of one's own body tissue without suicidal intent and for purposes not socially sanctioned. Common examples include cutting, burning, scratching, and banging or hitting. It was not the first time I had engaged in intentional self-harm, but it was certainly the scariest.

I've decided to write about this episode in my book and share my story to try to normalize the feelings associated with incidents like these, particularly when going through tough times.

We've been taught to repress, avoid, and hide any emotion that isn't positive or happy. The pressure to be perfect, and to keep our vulnerabilities hidden, can be overwhelming. I've certainly felt it.

From the outside, all people saw was a decently successful dude, running a company he was proud of, living with a swell girlfriend, loved by great parents, surrounded by amazing friends, and about to move into a new home. And that wasn't an accident.

Over the previous two years, I'd just promoted those achievements, and the compliments kept rolling in. But somewhere along the way, I stopped believing those compliments.

I began to dismiss each positive message, writing it off as someone giving thanks to the experience I helped provide, and not to me, the actual human who facilitated it. I convinced myself that if any of our attendees actually knew who I was as a person, they wouldn't be complimenting me.

How could people be praising me when all that circled in my brain were the bad things I had done in life? I ruminated on the times I manipulated others, the times I slammed metaphorical doors in people's faces, the times that I lied or made up stories about people. My self-loathing drowned out any positivity, as it always had—even during the best of times.

But what made it worse this time was that I extolled the benefits of gratitude—the impact of compassion and appreciation all day long—when I couldn't show myself the same courtesy. I had stopped believing in the magic.

I knew all of the things I needed to do to maintain a clear purpose and perspective, but I wasn't actually practicing them.

Meanwhile, with so much on-paper success, people began sharing advice and expectations to help me scale the heck out of our company. I began smothering under the overwhelm of more. I mean, hadn't we done enough?

I started to prioritize looking busy over being productive, valuing deals instead of the relationships behind them. I #hustled hard, and developed emotional impotence as a result.

I'd replaced what I'd originally fallen in love with at our experiences—co-creating safe spaces and meeting wonderful people—with recording profits and trying to "go bigger." And then I began to buy into my own hype, valuing social climbing and monetary wealth over the well-being of myself and others.

Yes, I was more successful on paper. But that monetary success was coming at the expense of things far more important to me: my deeply held values, personal connections, and a sense of play—all of which are directly connected to the soul.

Mother Teresa once noted what she called the deep poverty of the soul that afflicts the wealthy—and that the poverty of the soul in America was deeper than any poverty she had seen anywhere else on Earth. I had architected a life of scarcity and competition, rather than one of joy and abundance, and found myself in the depths of soul poverty as a result.

My friend Scott said that I had so many things going on that I couldn't see the forest for the trees.

When you feel like a monster, or you're going through hard times, or you're even overwhelmed with opportunity, it's easy to lose track of what's going well in your life. It's easy to want more constantly. It's easy to compare yourself with others. It's easy to stop believing what people tell you.

And so, as our company and impact were rising to new heights, I self-destructed. As I mentioned on December 30th, 2021, I hurt myself.

It was my cry for help, but I almost brought the whole ship down with me in the process. As bad as it felt to have done it, it felt even worse knowing that I almost brought down those I loved with me. My girlfriend, Molly, who was with me in person.

My mother and father, whom I called immediately afterward. My dearest friends, who were with me physically and spiritually in the days that followed (you know who you are). My team, and their financial well-being.

The situation, as complex as it was to create, was far simpler to explain. I had stopped appreciating all the good things I had going on in my life. Instead, I had become too focused on the few things that were going wrong. The gratitude stopped flowing.

The term for a lack of gratitude is *ingratitude*, and I was chock full of it.

Little did I know, I wasn't alone. The plague of ingratitude has a long history, and I'd become just one of its many victims.

# The Plague of Ingratitude



In the year A.D. 60, the ancient Roman Empire was a place of great power and control, having conquered more than half the world. From the outside, it had all the markings of success—a powerful army, a democratic system of government, and the world's greatest economy. But some of the people on the inside knew that, beneath it all, was a society that would eventually crumble.

Lucius Annaeus Seneca, also known as Seneca the Elder, was an elder statesman who wrote a book called *De Beneficiis*, or *On Benefits*. In that book, he described the greatest plague to Roman society: that its people knew neither how to give nor receive a benefit, and that of all the vices to which Rome's citizens fell prey, none were as significant as ingratitude.

He said that amongst "homicides, tyrants, thieves, adulterers, ravishers, sacrilegious, traitors," there was nothing "worse than the ungrateful man." He explained that many of those crimes actually flowed from ingratitude, "without which hardly any great wickedness has ever grown to full stature."

Seneca would join the ranks of other great Stoic philosophers—men like Socrates, Aristotle, and Marcus Aurelius. They touted a way of life that maximizes positive emotions, minimizes negative ones, and helps individuals to hone the virtues of their character. And their writings live on, helping countless people develop the virtues and strength of character to live meaningful lives over the last few thousand years.

Their words continue to resonate with so many today, due in part to the fact that they wrote during hard times—much like the ones we're facing today.

They provided principles and strategies to overcome the obstacles that inevitably show up in our lives, regardless of the millenia from whence we came.

Marcus Aurelius was one of the last great emperors of Rome. As a ruler during the Antonine plague, he knew a thing or two about overcoming obstacles—and even finding the benefits they offered.

He said, "the mind adapts and converts to its own purposes the obstacle to our acting. The impediment to action advances action. What stands in the way becomes the way." It was his credo for tackling the challenges in front of him. He instructed us to use moments of adversity as part of our story.

That perspective is key to Stoicism, which Nassim Nicholas Taleb defines as principles that will help you "transform fear into prudence, pain into information, mistakes into initiation, and desire into undertaking."

The father of modern Stoicism, Ryan Holiday, says, "Stoicism is one of history's most effective formulas for overcoming every negative situation we may encounter in life. A formula for thriving not just in spite of whatever happens, but BECAUSE of IT."

We are plagued with uncertainty and challenged by factors that most of us haven't encountered in our lifetimes. But, as the great Stoics of every era have explained, the adversity we're facing in the world today is a great opportunity to overcome and come together.

My team and I argue that gratitude is an essential part of the equation. Gratitude will give you the resilience and sense of belonging necessary to overcome what ails you.

What happens without it?

We can look to Seneca's observation about gratitude and consider the downfall of the Roman Empire, which included political uprising, financial debt, social divide, class warfare, plagues, and fake news—issues that align with what we see in society today.

Mental illness is at an all-time high, and our social and emotional well-being has plummeted, wreaking havoc on connection, belonging, creativity, and more. We are lonelier and more disconnected than ever before.

And because of that sense of disconnection, many of us are too cowardly, or entitled, or careless to come together and support each other.

We've gotten so caught up in all that's gone wrong that we've forgotten to be grateful for all that's going right. If what Seneca said about gratitude is true, then we should probably do something different than the Romans. We've got to do the opposite. We've got to build cultures of gratitude.

Gratitude, in its simplest form, is the acknowledgement of the benefits you've received—some sort of value that others have bestowed upon you. As psychologist Robert Emmons explains, "Gratitude has been called not only the greatest of the virtues, but the parent of all others, the moral memory of mankind, the most passionate transformative force in the cosmos, the key that opens all doors, the quality that makes us and keeps us young."

Gratitude can heal our suffering and our broken relationships. It can inspire us to move toward each other, and forward as a society. It can help us thrive.

# The Struggle and the Solution

*"We think sometimes that poverty is only being hungry, naked and homeless. The poverty of being unwanted, unloved and uncared for is the greatest poverty. We must start in our own homes to remedy this kind of poverty."*
– Mother Teresa

Seneca and the Stoics weren't the only ones to recognize the plague of ingratitude. Scottish Enlightenment philosopher David Hume said, "ingratitude is the most horrible and unnatural crime that a person is capable of committing." German philosopher Immanuel Kant stated that "ingratitude is, quite simply, the essence of vileness." The Tamil people of South India have a term, *nandri ketta nai*, which loosely translates to "gratitude-lacking dog." It's considered the worst insult of all.

That was me, the gratitude-lacking dog.

But as I looked around, I realized that so many others had gotten caught up in the challenges and opportunities of a shifting world order. I learned, further, that I had much to be grateful for, and that though my troubles seemed overwhelming, a dose of daily gratitude would make a major difference in my life.

Maybe you've stopped practicing gratitude as well. Maybe you feel the truth of what I'm saying, that sometimes in life we focus more on what's going wrong rather than appreciating what's actually going right. The moments of trauma, conflict, and missed opportunities can outshine the overwhelming evidence of what a miracle it is just to be alive—and how much the people around us want us here.

In the weeks following my NSSI episode, I was a pile of confused, emotional, mush. I watched Nancy Meyers movies on repeat and cried through every scene. I teared up walking down the street, or palming the perfect lemons that sat in a bowl on my kitchen counter. My heart was broken, my self-compassion was at an all-time low, and now I had to feel the feelings I'd been putting off for months. It was dark in the hole I'd dug for myself, and the reminders that life was still happening around me—beautiful movie kitchens and fresh fruit included—were almost painful to the touch.

(You might be in that hole now, and if you are, you're not alone.)

But then I realized something important: therein lay my greatest opportunity. True connection doesn't come from pretending our lives are perfect. True connection comes from reaching out to others during our greatest time of need.

With that in mind, I stopped pretending like the episode didn't happen and decided to make it part of my story. I'd pack it up, take it with me, and head out to fall back in love with gratitude again. I'm still on that journey, and I want you to be a part of it too.

We can find benefits in the shittiest of circumstances, and we can do it through gratitude. And if we can give gratitude to the different circumstances we encounter—good and bad—we can make the most difficult times in our lives part of our life story. And from there, hopefully, we can have a positive impact on others.

It's time to take a moment to reflect on all the good stuff in our lives, and share it—authentically—with others. When we do, everyone benefits. But you don't have to take my word for it.

My team and I have spent the past few years listening authentically to how people have been feeling. At the start of each Virtual Gratitude Experience™, we'd ask a simple question: *What's one word or phrase that honestly describes how you feel right now?*

We posed this question to tens of thousands of people during the most challenging years of their lives. Some of them were quarantined alone, others were stuck quarantining with people they couldn't wait to get rid of. Fifty-five percent of those people reported a very negative emotion, like "overwhelmed," "sad," "nervous," "cautious," "anxious," or "lonely." These people were balancing their professional responsibilities, with their personal duties—just as you were—and they were tearing apart at the seams. They were struggling under what felt like an unbearable weight. They could put on their happy face to log onto work calls and pretend like things were hunky-dory. But when those calls ended, panic and exhaustion set in.

Perhaps it was the added pressure of pandemic life—or perhaps the pandemic just served as the straw that broke the camel's back—but on our calls, people admitted how they were truly feeling. I'd never seen that level of fear and uncertainty in my life. Part of it was that no one knew what would happen, and amidst all the loss—of people we loved, a life that looked familiar, and more—it was hard to find the positive in anything. And part of it was that we were just lonely as hell.

But in our virtual experiences, people would find each other. A person who felt overwhelmed would meet someone who felt anxious and see that they weren't alone. Someone who felt lonely could meet someone who felt sad, and they would find so many things in common, including their wishes for tomorrow.

Sometimes, the people in our experiences started off feeling happy, optimistic, or excited, even in the face of adversity. And when people who were feeling overwhelmed, anxious, or lonely met them, they could benefit from the positivity of their colleagues—and vice versa. Everyone would leave with more perspective, empathy, compassion, and optimism.

All the while, we were finding the data to back up what we were seeing play out in real time.

The age-old idea that taking a headstrong, individual approach will help us overcome life's greatest challenges—a perspective perpetuated by the likes of René de Cartes, Thomas Hobbes, and Sigmund Freud—is inherently flawed.

Rather than naturally self-interested, individualistic creatures, we are actually wired for connection. In his book, *The Age of Empathy*, primatologist and ethologist Frans de Waal explains that we were born to be part of communities. Those who didn't ran the risk of being cast aside and losing out on the protection and resources necessary for survival. Getting along with others kept us alive.

Meanwhile, the individualism that has become a hallmark of Western culture has led to a world more isolated, lonely, unfulfilled and disconnected than ever before. The distance we've designed has made us emotionally detached, which makes us have feelings of fear, mistrust, suspicion, and anxiety when relating to others.

Even the most socially connected and successful leaders feel pretty isolated today. Some of you have vast networks and a strong digital presence, and still feel a lack of emotional connection. Even your long-term relationships may lack the depth of authentic intimacy. You don't have to be alone to be lonely.

Your success may even be making you lonelier. According to Thomas Joiner, author of *Lonely at the Top*, people often neglect close social relations in favor of focusing on goals associated with making it big. But with so many opportunities for surface-level connection and little else, most of society is suffering from a lack of connection.

You've convinced yourself that, because you have a ton of followers on Instagram, contacts in your phone, and people on your team, you feel a genuine sense of connection. In reality, though, you probably don't know that much about most of the people in your network. You don't know the adversity they have experienced. You don't know what brings them authentic and genuine joy. You don't know about how they feel like they're hiding in plain sight.

We have a whole nation of lonely people, and it's killing us. According to United States Surgeon General Vivek Murthy, "loneliness is as strong a risk factor for illness and death as smoking, obesity, and high blood pressure," and with 52 percent of Americans reporting that they are lonely on a regular basis, we have a real problem on our hands.

Our friend Kasley Killam, a founder dedicated to addressing the loneliness epidemic and improving social health, elucidates the problem even further. She writes that, "In recent decades the number of people with zero confidants has tripled, and most adults do not belong to a local community group. Consequently, more than one-third of Americans over the age of forty-five report feeling lonely, with prevalence especially high among those under twenty-five and over sixty-five years old."

Meanwhile, studies show that when you have people in your life who care about you, you're less likely to catch a cold, suffer a stroke, get heart disease, or experience cognitive decline. One study at Harvard University, made popular by Robert Waldinger's TED Talk, followed hundreds of people for seventy-five years—over the span of their lifetime—to determine some of the greatest predictors of a high quality of life. They found that the strength of their relationships was the greatest predictor of all.

And you can build those relationships through gratitude.

True, deep meaningful human connection is like a diamond . . . it lasts forever. Cultivating it, though, is hard. It requires courage, bravery, and unyielding vulnerability. But the shine through the mine erases the poverty of the soul.

We believe you can use gratitude to overcome trauma, to ease conflict, to improve your leadership, to build better teams and cultures, to enhance customer relationships, and leave a meaningful legacy—particularly during hard times. We'll show you how to do that here.

# What You'll Find in This Book

*"The beginning is the most important part of the work."*
– Plato

I've learned in books, and in practice, how gratitude can become a superpower, enabling you to overcome fear, failure, shame, and regret; get through your darkest hours; and find an immense sense of joy—one that is already in your heart and just within your reach.

Here, I'm sharing many of those insights with you, from the peer-reviewed studies on how gratitude reduces stress and anxiety, to the psychological theories at play when we give gratitude, and how to harness and share our appreciation so that it is felt by those around us for maximum impact. And you'll find real-world stories from successful founders and gratitude experts, Virtual Gratitude Experience™ attendees, and yours truly to drive it all home.

With that in mind, you'll notice that this book is broken down into sections, highlighting the scientific and psychological research behind gratitude, why gratitude is so effective during tough times, how to express gratitude effectively as an individual and as a leader more specifically, and the rituals to incorporate gratitude into your daily life. I hope you'll read through it from start to finish, and then return to it as needed, revisiting relevant sections on a regular basis.

In each section, you'll find *Gratitude Inquiries*—questions to help you identify and explore the impact of gratitude on your day-to-day life. Take five to ten minutes to answer these simple inquiries, and you'll quickly see how gratitude has the power to transform every facet of your world.

Know too, that we at 7:47 are here to support your gratitude journey. Consider this book Gratitude 101, the introductory course to a life-long education. When you're ready, we'll help you take the next step.

You'll find that gratitude is not only easy to incorporate as a practice and act upon in your daily life, but also contagious. When you learn how to genuinely care about yourself and others through gratitude, you'll be able to make peace with yourself and with the people you encounter, and set off a chain reaction of gratitude so powerful that you won't be able to track its full impact.

Along the way, you'll spark respect, caring, curiosity, and authenticity in your relationships, driving more fulfillment.

And by the time you're done reading, you'll find that the only thing standing in the way of a better existence is yourself, and a case of ingratitude.

Before we jump in, though, I want to take you through your first gratitude micro-intervention—the same one in which Virtual Gratitude Experience™ participants partake.

Grab a pen and a piece of paper (I'll wait).

***If you could give credit or thanks to one person in your life, that you don't give enough credit or thanks to, who would that be?***

Set a five-minute timer, and write down as many things about that person and your interactions as you can recollect. Here are a few questions to take you deeper, in case that's helpful:

- *Is the person living or dead?*
- *If they're living, do you still talk to them?*
- *Do you consider your relationship with them to be positive or negative?*
- *What have you learned from this person?*
- *What's their legacy?*
- *If they were here right now, what would you say to them?*
- *If you had to tell a story about them, what would you share?*

Now, take a deep breath and look over what you've written. Did anything that came up surprise you? How do you feel now?

I'm so darn excited to have you.

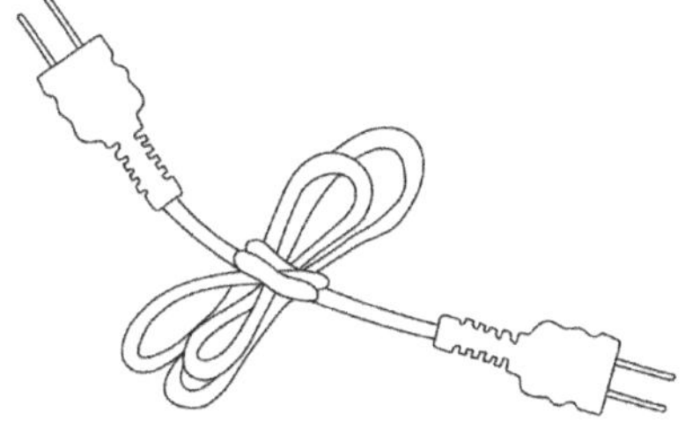

## PART I

# We're Wired for Connection

*"Wear gratitude like a cloak and it will
feed every corner of your life"*
– Rumi

# Gratitude Backed by History, Art, Psychology, and Science

*"A thankful heart is not only the greatest virtue,*
*but the parent of all the other virtues."*
– Cicero

You don't have to look hard to find historical insight on the value of gratitude. From the mysticism of Rumi to the stoicism of Marcus Aurelius, lines in praise of gratitude abound in the world of arts and letters.

For thousands of years, gratitude has been called not only the greatest of the virtues, but also the "moral memory of mankind," "the most passionate transformative force in the cosmos," "the key that opens all doors," and "the quality that makes us and keeps us young." Even the Roman statesman Cicero mentioned gratitude as the "mother" of all human feelings.

But gratitude can feel pretty fluffy at times. I've seen the regard in which it's held firsthand.

When I arrive in a company auditorium or—more often than not these days—appear on employee computer screens and mention that we'll be focusing on gratitude, I watch attendees roll their eyes or begin side-bar chats with colleagues. And I understand why: gratitude has been cast as religious and spiritual filler, or a promise-filled product shilled by a multi-billion dollar self-help industry that cares more about cashing out than truly cultivating well-being.

It's easy to feel that gratitude has nothing to offer us, especially when life feels so dang difficult.

But over the past century, we've come to understand that the benefits of gratitude are more than a fleeting feel-good feeling. Gratitude is fuel for our minds, bodies, and organizations, a reality that has been corroborated time and again.

Whether captured in battle-tested philosophies from thought leaders past and present, or research from pioneers like Barbara Fredrickson, Chester Elton, Robert Emmons, Steven Kotler, and Marty Seligman, giving gratitude is widely recognized as an evidence-based intervention with the power to affect physiology and psychology in big ways.

When we're going through tough times, it's the secret sauce to turn negatives into positives, decrease anxiety, inspire action, and trigger flow. As we begin our journey to understand why gratitude is so important, let's delve into the science and psychology that support gratitude as one of the best tools we have for personal, organizational, and societal improvement.

Before we jump in, I must note that I'm not a counselor or therapist. But the findings in this book are from expert researchers, and the interventions I share can be performed without support from a trained professional—typically in a short period of time. The length of this book and the sections within are designed to mimic the shortness of time gratitude takes to seep into your soul and change your life.

You don't need a PhD, or even a master's degree, to access the benefits of gratitude by incorporating some simple practices into your daily life. They are free, easy, immediate, and impactful.

You also don't need to know it all. There are thousands of studies delineating the positive benefits of gratitude, but for the sake of time, I'll only focus on a handful here. You'll find that, even in this small cross section, the evidence is overwhelming: Gratitude is transformative.

## Gratitude Inquiry:

- *Reflection: What is your first memory of being grateful for something or someone?*

- *Reflection: What reservations or hesitations do you have about gratitude at this point in time (if any)?*

- *Action: Purchase a book written by one of the people I mentioned in this section.*

# Gratitude Broadens and Builds Positive Emotions

*"Gratitude opens your heart and carries the urge
to give back—to do something good in return, either for
the person who helped you or for someone else."*
– Barbara Fredrickson

My friend Emily Fletcher is the author of *Stress Less, Accomplish More* and the founder of Ziva, a renowned meditation studio in New York City. She describes gratitude as a "natural antidepressant."

Emily explains that gratitude practices—like meditation—do more than just lower stress hormones. They rewire the brain at the neurotransmitter level to produce feelings of happiness and contentment.

Practicing gratitude releases the neurotransmitters serotonin and dopamine, which are crucial for pleasure and effective decision-making. They also improve our mood. That's especially vital in our current age, when our handheld technology keeps the twenty-four-hour news cycle just one swipe away, dominating our attention and depleting our serotonin and dopamine levels at a rapid pace. Gratitude allows us to slow down enough to replenish those levels. But the benefits don't stop there.

Practicing gratitude doesn't just provide a quick boost; it has lasting effects on the brain.

Emily writes that, "The more you stimulate these neural pathways through practicing gratitude, the stronger and more automatic they become. On a scientific level, this is an example of Hebb's Law, which states 'neurons that fire together wire together.' The more times a certain neural pathway is activated (neurons firing together), the less effort it takes to stimulate the pathway the next time (neurons wiring together)." As such, what we attend to grows, much like a garden. Give attention to how often you are grateful, and you'll find yourself feeling grateful more frequently—even when you're not putting effort toward the practice.

Research psychologist Barbara Fredrickson explained that, in addition to gratitude's role as a mood enhancer, it can also alter thought-action tendencies.

Fredrickson defines a thought-action tendency as, "a learned tendency to evaluate things in a certain way." In other words, are you a glass half-full or glass half-empty kind of thinker? Optimists will be the ones who attest that the glass is half-full, whereas pessimists usually point out that it's half-empty.

How do you perceive the world around you, particularly during hard times?

Some of us roam the earth with a narrow and negative set of thought tendencies like fear, anger, resentment, and envy. As a result, we're primed to escape, attack, thwart, and so on. And with good reason. Those narrow and negative thought-action tendencies served our ancestors well thousands of years ago when they faced life-threatening situations. Anger helped us fight to kill and fear enabled us to flee or outfox predators. It's why we're here today. The problem is, we don't need to avoid lions and tigers anymore. We live in neighborhoods and work in office buildings devoid of the threat of wild animals, yet these tendencies have remained, and today they typically create more harm than good.

According to Fredrickson's Broaden and Build theory, negative emotions like those associated with fear, anger, envy, or resentment create a narrow thought-action repertoire. A narrow thought-action repertoire is similar to having blinders on in your life. Lingering negative emotions can rob you of long-term growth by preventing you from seeing opportunities and potential.

While negative emotions create a narrow thought-action repertoire, positive emotions do the opposite: they broaden our thought-action repertoire and expand the horizons of what is possible in our lives. Fredrickson says that "broadened mindsets carry indirect and long-term adaptive benefits because broadening builds enduring personal resources, which function as reserves to be drawn on later to manage future threats."

Joy, she says, can broaden our repertoire by creating the urge to play, be creative, and be more socially inclined. Interest broadens our repertoire by creating the urge to explore new information and experiences, enabling us to expand our knowledge in the process. Pride broadens by encouraging us to share our achievements with others, while helping us envision a brighter future for ourselves. Contentment lets us savor our current life and integrate our understanding of ourselves and what we know about the world. These positive emotions enhance our ability to think about what's possible, and find joy in that vision—which is directly related to an increase in dopamine levels. And importantly, they have the ability to "undo" the lingering effects of negative emotions.

How does all this connect to gratitude?

When we express gratitude, our thought-action repertoires broaden, literally rewiring our brains.

That means we are able to think and act flexibly, in ways that take into account the bigger picture, a broader periphery. Over time, the effects of gratitude accumulate and compound. The result is that we can see an ever-increasing number of ways to solve problems and bounce back. And solving problems more effectively in the first place means we need to tap into our personal reserves less frequently.

Frederickson says that "gratitude arises when an individual perceives that another person has acted intentionally to improve the beneficiary's well-being." When people are grateful they usually show it, which forms social bonds and friendship and encourages them to pay it forward.

The more frequently we feel grateful and show gratitude, the higher our baseline of well-being and the less frequently it's diminished. Over time, these effects of gratitude accumulate and compound. The result is access to an ever-increasing number of ways to solve problems and bounce back from setbacks—all while spending less of our personal resources to do so and enriching the lives of others.

So, go do something that brings you joy and stimulates your creativity. Then, show gratitude for the experience and watch what happens.

## Gratitude Inquiry:

- *Reflection: Do you consider yourself a glass half-full or glass half-empty-type thinker? And Why?*

- *Reflection: What's an example of something (an emotion, action, or perspective) that felt challenging at first, but became easier over time? This is an example of broadening thought-action repertoire!*

- *Action: Write down three actions that have brought you joy or pride over the years. Complete one this week!!*

# Gratitude Fuels
# Hope and Healing

*"The struggle ends when gratitude begins."*
– Neale Donald Walsch

The majority of people approach gratitude as a treatment for what ails them. "I'll get out my gratitude journal when I'm having a bad day so that I no longer feel sad," they think. They practice gratitude in one-off settings to boost their mood rather than view gratitude as a way to prevent loneliness, exhaustion, heart disease, and so much more.

Gratitude is a vitamin, not a pill. Vitamins keep your systems running optimally. You don't necessarily perceive their impact if everything is well-regulated. You take a pill to treat an illness that is already established. If you miss a dose, you're right back to feeling awful. Gratitude doesn't work in pill form. It works like preventive medicine.

Most types of Western medicine focus on treating an illness or injury, rather than keeping the ailment from happening. The idea with preventive medicine is that it stops sickness before it begins through promoting health and well-being. Much like preventive medicine, gratitude isn't something you do occasionally to feel better. It requires that you put the work in every day.

The good news is that the work is worth it. If gratitude could be bottled up and sold in a pharmacy, no one would be able to keep it in stock. An article published by the UC Davis Medical Center outlines an incredible list of health benefits to giving gratitude that have been shown in a number of studies:

- Gratitude is related to a 10 percent improvement in sleep quality in patients with chronic pain, 76 percent of whom had insomnia, and 19 percent lower depression levels

- A daily gratitude practice can decelerate the effects of neurodegeneration (as measured by a 9 percent increase in verbal fluency) that occurs with increasing age

- Practicing gratitude led to a 7 percent reduction in biomarkers of inflammation in patients with congestive heart failure

- Grateful people have 16 percent lower diastolic blood pressure and 10 percent lower systolic blood pressure compared to those who weren't as grateful

- Grateful people (including people grateful to God) had 9–13 percent lower levels of Hemoglobin A1c, a key marker of glucose control that plays a significant role in the diagnosis of diabetes

Now *those* are the kinds of side effects I'd want to hear in a pharmaceutical commercial.

Gratitude can enhance your ability to heal.

Studies have shown that gratitude has emerged as one of the strongest themes for a quality of life following an invasive surgery, like an organ transplant. I've seen gratitude's impact on healing first-hand.

My girlfriend, Molly, has a sister named Hope. Hope was born less than a year after Molly, yet they had incredibly different childhood experiences. Hope was born with Spina Bifida and Chiari malformation. She has had hundreds of surgeries in her life, and uses a wheelchair. She's also a childhood cancer survivor. And she is a beacon of gratitude, even in tough times.

When Hope was a kid, her doctors commented that she was able to recover more quickly than anyone they'd ever seen in the pediatric cancer unit. They thought her grateful attitude played a huge part in her healing.

When the COVID-19 pandemic required us to pivot from in-person events to Virtual Gratitude Experiences™, I had the opportunity to invite Hope to a number of them. She struggled the first time I asked her our Signature Gratitude Question: ***If you could give credit or thanks to one person in your life, that you don't give enough credit or thanks to, who would that be?***

It was difficult for her to figure out who she had never thought to thank because she has been grateful for everybody and made a point of showing it. Gratitude is her default, and that's a pretty powerful setting. Eventually, she began thanking her eight brothers and sisters for various experiences in their lives, and kept repeating the cycle.

# Gratitude Inquiry:

- *Reflection: What are some preventative measures that you currently practice to look after your health (mental, physical, emotional?)*


- *Reflection: What symptoms are you currently experiencing and would like to be free of? Examples could include anxiety, insomnia, heartbreak, loneliness, exhaustion, etc.*


- *Action: Based on the research shared in this chapter, envision what health benefits you would like to experience in your life as a result of gratitude. The sky's the limit!*

# Gratitude Triggers Flow



Gratitude not only creates lasting structural change within the brain and body, it also fundamentally changes behavior. Back in the 1970s, psychologist Mihaly Csikszentmihalyi coined the term "flow" to describe an altered state of consciousness, a place where every single moment and decision cascaded seamlessly from the last.

At the time, Csikszentmihalyi was studying the peak performance rituals of tens of thousands of people around the world. He asked them about the times when they felt or performed their best in their craft, whether that be sports, gaming, business, or farming.

Every single person answered that they felt their best when they were in the state he'd come to define as flow. He found flow could alter their sense of time, vanish their sense of self, and give them complete concentration. This magical consciousness had the power to inspire individuals to perform to the best of their ability at whatever they were doing—and to feel great doing it.

Flow can also help erase the negativity bias that often stands in the way of accomplishing great things. According to author Kendra Cherry, "Negativity bias is our tendency not only to register negative stimuli more readily but also to dwell on unfortunate events. Also known as positive-negative asymmetry, this negativity bias means that we feel the sting of a rebuke more powerfully than we feel the joy of praise."

In short, if something bad happened in our past, we expect it to happen again. You stubbed your toe once, you're going to stub it again. A friend disappointed you once, so others will do the same thing. Negativity bias also explains why the challenge of trying to fix a few tough things in your life may feel much more present than the abundance of positive experiences you've had (that's certainly the case for me).

Gratitude can help. The world's current leading expert on peak performance, *New York Times* bestselling author and Pulitzer Prize nominee Steven Kotler has explored the connection between gratitude and flow. *In The Art of the Impossible: A Peak Performance Primer*, he writes that there appears to be a strong link between gratitude and a high-flow lifestyle.

To understand the power of what he learned, you've got to understand a bit of evolutionary biology. Kotler references an experiment run at the University of California, Berkeley, in which psychologists found that we process as many as nine bits of negative information for every positive bit that gets through. That negative programming is what kept us safe in our primal days roaming the plain. Unfortunately, as I mentioned, in a world virtually devoid of such risks, the negative information we take in just leads to crippling anxiety and stress—and can ultimately alter our life's course.

But we don't have to get stuck in all that negativity. Kotler found that "a daily gratitude practice alters the brain's negativity bias. It changes the amygdala's filter, essentially training it to take in more positive information. This works so well because the positive stuff you're grateful for is stuff that has already happened. It never trips our bullshit detector."

Further, Kotler's Flow Research Collective, a research and training institute designed to help people reach peak performance, and USC neuroscientist Glenn Fox found that "the optimism and confidence that was produced by gratitude lowered people's anxiety. When we have less anxiety, we are less fearful of stretching to the edge of our abilities and more able to target the *challenge-skills sweet spot*, flow's most important trigger."

Challenge-skills sweet spots represent the perfect balance between the stuff that's too boring to hold our attention, and that which is too difficult to keep us in the game. These challenge-skills sweet spots trigger flow because they demand task-specific focus, and I'll argue that gratitude requires task-specific focus.

That flow induces joy, and joy sparks the urge to play. It induces positive feelings that far outweigh any frustrations you may be attempting to overcome. And that means you'll have so much more to be grateful for!

There were many factors that led to my NSSI in late 2021, but I know for certain that a lack of flow was among them. At the time of my episode, I just couldn't reach that challenge-skills sweet spot. There were some parts of my life that were too challenging, like 7:47's extraordinarily rapid growth and the fact that I'd taken on way too many projects. And there were other parts of my life that had become so routine that they felt boring, like producing the same kinds of experiences over and over again. As a result, my life fell into complete disarray.

Even when we're going through extremely difficult times, we can still find benefits in the situation at hand. I couldn't. It's because I was plagued by ingratitude.

If I had taken the time to be grateful, I could have identified what was working and what wasn't and adjusted accordingly.

Let gratitude help you find your challenge-skills sweet spots and set you up to flow.

## Gratitude Inquiry:

- *Reflection: When was the last time you felt in flow? What did you experience in that state? What activities became effortless?*

- *Reflection: What are some past memories that you currently have a negative association with? How could these memories inhibit your ability to access a dedicated flow state?*

- *Action: Choose an area of your life where you want to experience more flow and describe how it meets the challenge-skills sweet spot: something that isn't too hard or too easy. Eliminate one thing in your life this week so you can focus more on living in that flow.*

# Gratitude Limits Entitlement

*"Humility isn't thinking less of yourself,*
*it's thinking of yourself less."*
– C.S. Lewis

A huge part of finding success in work and life is acknowledging that you have something to learn, not only from the world but also from others. When we fail to realize that, entitlement rears its ugly head. We end up believing we deserve privileges or special treatment inherently. Entitlement is essentially a "you owe me" attitude. It occurs as a result of the way we were raised, the way we grew up in society, how authority treats us, and more.

We've all known entitled people. Most entitled people are in perpetual state of unhappiness, conflict, disappointment, and depression.

The question is, how often do we acknowledge our own entitlement?

Think about the last time you were in conflict with someone. Often, when we are in conflict with others, we look at ourselves in one of two ways: as superior, or as a victim.

When we feel superior, we imagine ourselves to be more important, virtuous, and in the right. Meanwhile, we see them as inferior, morally questionable, and flat-out wrong. As a result, we are impatient and disdainful. And while it may feel good to see yourself as better than someone else in the short term, it can lead to more tension, as well as disappointment, depression, and unhappiness.

We can also walk through the world feeling like a victim—unappreciated and mistreated by those we encounter. We may believe what we've been through is bigger than what others have experienced, making us feel deprived and resentful. We convince ourselves that our trauma is the biggest trauma anyone in our community has experienced, and we are thus deserving of special attention. The world appears to be both unjust and to owe us something. That's where that "I deserve" mentality comes in, which can be damaging to our motivation and success in the long run.

Both of these mindsets produce entitlement.

Our self-perspective—and thus our sense of entitlement—develops in a variety of ways. Some of us grow up expecting that life will look a certain way. We believe that we'll accomplish everything we desire, and we'll be showered with accolades along the way. These messages are reinforced by the culture we're a part of and the media we consume—movies, books, and social media. They are reinforced by our parents, awards through school and sports, and the prophecies in our yearbook superlatives. We become so used to our visions of what our lives will be like that we expect that they'll happen almost automatically. We believe we're entitled to them.

Gratitude creates humility, which is essentially the opposite of entitlement. **Giving gratitude is the act of acknowledging**

**that you've received some sort of benefit in your life from someone else.** That acknowledgement reinforces the fact that you didn't get here alone, and shifts the focus to the people who have helped you along the way.

When we are humble, we acknowledge that while we may have great abilities, we must rely on others—and we think about those people first.

Adam Grant writes about "otherish" people in his book, *Give and Take*. Otherish people are givers; they want to help others. But that doesn't mean they don't care about themselves. In fact, he explains that "they also have ambitious goals for advancing their own interests." He says that maintaining this posture of otherness will help reorient our perspective by identifying what it means to live generously in a sustainable manner to others, rather than just for ourselves—without losing awareness of what we need.

The result? Success without entitlement, which is more fulfilling and sustainable for you and better for society. In other words, it's otherish.

## Gratitude Inquiry:

- *Reflection: How do you feel when you spend time around an entitled person?*

- *Reflection: When have you experienced feeling superior in a situation? What might have been available if you had adopted a posture of gratitude and humility instead?*

- *Action: Write down two names of people you feel a sense of entitlement towards, either because you feel superior to or less than. Reach out to them this week from a place of humility and tell them a few things you've learned from them or how they've impacted your life.*

# Gratitude Promotes Presence

*"True happiness is to enjoy the present, without
anxious dependence upon the future, not to amuse ourselves
with either hopes or fears but to rest satisfied with what
we have, which is sufficient, for he that so wants nothing.
The greatest blessings of mankind are within us and
within our reach. A wise man is content with his lot,
whatever it may be, without wishing for what he has not."*
– Seneca

Life may be a lot different than it was during Roman Stoic Seneca's day, but we'd do well to heed his wise words—particularly in an age when so many of us default to anxiety. We're so consumed with what's going to happen, that we forget to live in the present. The problem with that, particularly in a world that is in constant flux thanks to today's breakneck pace of information, is that it's virtually impossible to know where we're going to be tomorrow.

A while ago, I asked my friend Cheryl a simple question—the same one my team and I have asked attendees at the start of every Virtual Gratitude Experience™ since the beginning of the pandemic. "What's one word that honestly describes how you feel right now?" I asked.

"Anxious," she said. Her nanny had just quit after six years. As a full-time executive at a big company, Cheryl led a team of hundreds. And now she'd have to figure out how to shoulder all of the duties of a stay-at-home parent too.

She didn't know which direction to take the company, how to cover the tasks her nanny had managed, how to manage her time, or how to make space for her own well-being amidst it all.

But as we talked, I realized there was a deeper anxiety at play. It wasn't just about how to get it all done; it was that she wasn't sure she trusted herself to be a good mother. She had always had help, and now she was going at it alone. What if she failed, and her child resented her for the rest of her life? The revelation was powerful, emotional, vulnerable, and real.

When she'd laid it all out on the table, I invited her to practice a moment of gratitude.

"What are you grateful for right now?" I asked.

"Honestly, the ability to spend so much time with my child," Cheryl responded.

Rather than working eight hours a day in an office, plus logging an hour-long commute each way, she was handling it all from home. That meant she had much more facetime with her kid.

Yes, the majority of her day was still spent doing her job, keeping the company strategy afloat while covering the bills. But she also had two to three more hours of quality time with her child each day, during the most formative years of their life. That's hundreds of hours per year!

When I pointed that out to her, she broke down into tears. What had started off a few minutes prior as anxiety had shifted into gratitude, and then into a major sense of relief. The feeling was visible on her face. I encouraged her to go hug her child right then (when we pause to practice gratitude, we reap massive benefits)!

Prior to our talk, her expectations of who she was and how she had to live had led her to a state of misery when the conditions of her life inevitably changed. When her plans went awry, she was too focused on the future—all that *would* happen—to see the opportunity in front of her, right then and there. When we live too much in the future, we forget to look around and appreciate the agility of the moment we're in. Stepping into the present enables you to experience the benefits of contentment, peace, and rest—all of which opens the door for reflection and satisfaction.

When you're more present thanks to gratitude, you're less worried about what's to come—for example, death.

One experiment put this concept to the test. Researchers divided eighty-three adults over the age of sixty into three groups. One group was asked to write gratitude notes. Another group was asked to write about their greatest worries in life. And the third group was asked to write about something neutral. After the writing exercise, all of them were exposed to media clips filled with anxiety-inducing scenes focused on death.

After watching, the participants in the gratitude group had less death anxiety than the other two groups.

Why?

The exercise brought them into the present, and as a result they were less afraid of the future. Scientifically speaking, gratitude has an impact on the sympathetic nervous system, which activates our anxiety responses. It conditions the brain to let go of negative ruminations and focus on positive thoughts, namely, what we're grateful for.

Seneca said, "we suffer more in imagination than in reality." When we feel anxious, we must remind ourselves that we're responding to something that hasn't happened—something that's not really there. We torture ourselves thinking about the "what if," rather than appreciating what's actually going on. We can act on his advice—"do not be unhappy before the crisis comes,"—with a little help from gratitude.

To be truly grateful for our present moment is to genuinely be at peace with time. As I'm writing this, I am grateful that I do not feel the overwhelming pressure of more. I am grateful to know at this moment I've done enough. I'm grateful to sit on this couch and slowly re-read this passage with my girlfriend.

## Gratitude Inquiry:

- *Reflection: What are 3-5 things on your to-do list or schedule that feel like busywork and keep you from being present?*

- *Reflection: What future events do you find yourself worrying about?*

- *Action: Identify an experience in the present moment that you can be grateful for - right here, right now. Observe how this simple act of writing down your gratitude brings you into a state of presence and peace.*

# Gratitude Sparks Serendipity

*"I'm thankful for serendipitous moments in my life,
where things could've gone the other way."*
– Rick Springfield

When my team and I launched our Virtual Gratitude Experiences™ in 2020, they had an accidental theme: serendipity.

Pre-pandemic, serendipity was all around. We found it with the doorman when we left our apartments, with strangers in the coffee line, and with colleagues at the water cooler. These blissful but fleeting moments of connection made us feel less alone, and they were so easy to come by that most—if not all—of us took them for granted. When the pandemic hit, we lost those moments of serendipity. We lost the opportunity to go out and have random, chance encounters with people we knew and those we didn't.

But our Virtual Gratitude Experiences™ brought those moments back. When we brought people together via virtual breakout groups, they got to connect with strangers, acquaintances, and close friends alike.

Through our breakout groups, we introduced background knowledge into these connections. In small groups, our participants explained the background of their lives through gratitude, giving credit and thanks to people from their past. When someone shared a story about the third grade teacher who taught them about the subject that became their life's work, they provided background knowledge. That extra information often inspired others to think about the teachers in their lives, and to realize that *they* had a teacher who introduced them to something just as powerful.

Often, participants found themselves in the first serendipitous encounter they'd experienced in weeks or even months. Many of them had been so focused on surviving until the next day, they forgot how good a small, random chat could feel—the kind they used to have with a barista or coworker. Our pandemic routines had smothered serendipity and the commonality that comes with it, and as a result, they had been suffocating.

Our dear friend Zvi Band says, "Progress in all aspects of our lives—and the world around us—relies on breaking out of the routine. Meeting different people, being exposed to different ideas, gives us the medium upon which to change our thinking and ultimately, grow."

When we realize all that we have in common, through moments of serendipity, we find connection. This connection sparks joy. It fills us with positive emotions we may not have known we were missing. And so our attendees found common ground not in a shared apartment building or office but in a Zoom room.

Over the course of the pandemic, I got to witness brilliant moments of serendipity. I saw two men—one stationed in India and another in the US—who had nothing in common on paper give gratitude for the mothers that had never told them they loved them. I watched as two people in the same breakout group discovered that they were both authors and executive coaches quarantining in Montclair, New Jersey—a realization that came about when they both gave gratitude to their neighbors. And I experienced my own powerful moment of serendipity, thanks to my regular newsletter.

Throughout my life, I've made a point of honoring my paternal grandfather and namesake, Chris Schembra.

Papa, as I called him, was a Sicilian butcher who gave my family its start in America. But I hadn't given much thought to my paternal grandmother, Luise Infante Schembra, whose family immigrated from just outside of Salerno. In my newsletter a few years ago, I mentioned how grateful I was for the life they'd built together.

About two hours later, I received a text from a friend I'd known for a few years. We'd worked alongside each other at Soho House, and spent some time chatting about business. "I didn't know you were an Infante!' it read.

After some digging, we realized that our grandparents were from tiny neighboring towns of about 200 people each. It was a beautiful moment of serendipity that only unfolded because I took some time to give gratitude to someone I'd never thought to thank.

There's a Latin phrase: *amor fati*, fate in the universe. If you put people in a room together and ask them what and who they're grateful for, they'll find it: moments of serendipity that help keep them afloat.

It's up to us to set the scene for serendipity. What would happen if you surrendered any expectations you have in a particular setting? Would serendipitous points of connection pop up in front of your eyes? Have those points of connection been there all along and we just never gave ourselves the chance to see them?

## Gratitude Inquiry:

- *Reflection: What serendipitous encounters have you had recently and what did you learn?*

- *Reflection: When is the last time you connected with someone that you perceived to have nothing in common with, only to find you share a simple and serendipitous story or emotion in common?*

- *Action: Do one small thing today to allow yourself more serendipity in your day-to-day life. For instance, put your phone away while you're waiting in line for coffee.*

# Gratitude Makes Life Worth Living

*"The aim of Positive Psychology is to catalyze a change in psychology from a preoccupation only with repairing the worst things in life to also building the best qualities in life."*
– Martin Seligman

Here at 7:47, we are massive fans of the positive psychology movement. While much of the field of psychology focuses on identifying and treating mental illness, positive psychology focuses on traits, thinking patterns, behaviors, and experiences that help people improve the way they show up in the world and live long, happy, and successful lives.

The father of it all is Marty Seligman, a renowned professor at the University of Pennsylvania. By combining Abraham Maslow's hierarchy of needs, Eric Erickson's seven stages of psychosocial development, and dozens of other fundamental frameworks, Seligman established a field of study that digs into what makes life worth living. And fortunately, you don't have to be a trained clinician to practice positive psychology.

The basic tenet of positive psychology is that we must fully understand the human experience—the peaks, the valleys, and everything in between—to live life to its fullest. Seligman suggests that we follow a series of positive psychological interventions to help us do so. These interventions include empathy-building activities, optimism-inspiring activities, kindness boosters, gratitude interventions, and more. His vision is that these interventions create a powerful existence that encompasses six core virtues: wisdom, courage, humanity, justice, temperance, and transcendence.

One virtue in particular is of great importance to us at 7:47, and that is the virtue of transcendence. Transcendence helps us connect to the universe at large and live a life of meaning, purpose, and service to others. In 1971, Abraham Maslow defined transcendence as, "the very highest and most inclusive or holistic levels of human consciousness, behaving and relating to oneself, to significant others, to human beings in general, to other species, to nature, and to the cosmos." It's the virtue at the very top of his hierarchy of needs.

To us, the key concept that catches our attention is "relating . . . to human beings in general." If we can find a way to effectively relate to others, we will find meaning, connection, and purpose.

Each of the virtues Seligman outlined contain a subset of three to five character strengths. Well, one of the character strengths underneath the virtue of transcendence is gratitude.

I've always believed that no character strength has a more significant impact on well-being than gratitude, but Seligman's trials provide the evidence.

In 2005, Seligman and his team invited 577 individuals to participate in a multi-month study. There were six different conditions, with one control group and five interventions. One group's participants made a list of their individual strengths, one wrote down three things that made them unique, another group engaged in a gratitude visit, and so on.

Those in the gratitude visit group were tasked with writing a letter of gratitude to someone in their lives and then hand-delivering it to a recipient. Rather than a self-reflective activity, like writing in a gratitude journal that never sees the light of day, this act of gratitude was *prosocial*, a behavior meant to benefit others.

Seligman and his team were trying to determine whether the act would increase happiness and decrease depressive symptoms for those writing and delivering the letters.

The results were outstanding. At the one-week and one-month marks post-intervention, participants in the gratitude visit condition showed the most significant positive changes, compared to the other groups.

The study offered evidence that gratitude can have a lasting impact, transforming from short-term mood to long-term disposition with the right positive psychology intervention. And those with grateful dispositions tend to remain grateful in all seasons—good and bad (remember Molly's sister, Hope?). Think of that grateful disposition as an armor against resentment, envy, and self-loathing.

Keep in mind, though, that maintaining the benefits of gratitude takes ongoing effort. Participants in the gratitude visit group returned to their pre-intervention baseline after three months. That means that gratitude must be practiced on a regular basis to keep the good vibes alive. It's like the old saying goes, "You use it, or you lose it."

Don't lose it.

# Gratitude Inquiry:

- *Reflection: According to positive psychology, a powerful existence encompasses six core virtues: wisdom, courage, humanity, justice, temperance, and transcendence. Which of these values are present in your life? Which do you want more access to?*

- *Reflection: What's the first thing you think of when you hear the word "transcendence?" Have you had an experience of transcendence before?*

- *Action: Write a letter of gratitude to someone and hand-deliver it this week! Observe how long you feel the ripple effect of gratitude afterwards.*

# The Benefits of Belonging

*"Love and compassion are
necessities, not luxuries. Without them,
humanity cannot survive."*
– Dalai Lama XIV

# Building Bridges to Belonging



Belonging is a fundamental human need that is hardwired into our DNA. When we're going through trying times, it's easy to feel like we don't belong. We imagine we're the only ones who are having that particular experience. And rather than seeking out a community, we tend to isolate ourselves further. In fact, 40 percent of people say they feel isolated at work, resulting in lower organizational engagement and commitment.

To understand where this sense of isolation comes from, we must first consider the alternative. Belonging is defined as "the feeling of security and support when there is a sense of acceptance, inclusion, and identity for a member of a certain group or place." That doesn't mean your life needs to be filled with like-minded individuals; it means that everyone around you must accept you or be accepted for who they are.

Let me restate that concept in different words: belonging is not about building a group of others like you. It's about finding people who accept you for who you are—even if they are completely different from you. This is especially true in the workplace.

As Brene Brown says, "True belonging doesn't require you to change who you are; it requires you to be who you are."

Our friend Karen Mangia, bestselling author and Vice President of Customer and Market Insights at Salesforce, drives this point home with her take: "Belonging is bonding. Belonging is not blending."

Studies show that it's not their connection to an organization's mission or vision that keeps people engaged at work, it's genuine connection to the *people* around them—their sense of belonging. High belonging is linked to a 56 percent improvement in job performance, a 50 percent drop in turnover risk, and a 75 percent reduction in sick days taken.

But belonging isn't a concept or skill you can develop through training—it's a human experience. Many leaders get this wrong, expecting their teams to bond over key points delivered in workshops and webinars and overlooking the unique opportunity to *feel* together.

After engaging with hundreds of companies, my team and I have learned that creating deep and robust human connection is the secret ingredient for long-term belonging. The most effective way to inspire leaders is through their hearts and personal values. By bringing together leaders and diverse teams for an immersive journey into belonging, we build bridges and create allies at all levels of an organization. The safe space we build is a playground for people to share their stories, find common ground, and commit to co-create a culture of connection for the long run.

Through honest dialogue in safe spaces, people can experience empathy and gratitude—elements of connection that help them feel what it means to belong. When gratitude is expressed on a group level, it strengthens relationships and increases pro-social behavior, job satisfaction, and productivity. This foundation of gratitude and connection is the relational gel that builds support and continued engagement.

Of course, the benefits go beyond the professional to the personal. The people on your team feel seen, heard, connected, and supported as individuals. It's a pivotal shift that reduces loneliness and motivates people to expand their circle to encompass others. That, in and of itself, can be life-changing. And it can happen in a place where few expect to experience it: at work.

At one of our Virtual Gratitude Experiences™, a woman named Christina shared an interesting starting emotion. When we asked how people were feeling at the beginning of the session, she responded with "low confidence."

The next step was to enter a virtual breakout room with a partner, and discuss their starting emotions in greater detail for six minutes. Christina was paired with a woman on her team she had never met before. In that breakout room, "low-confidence" Christina met "anxious" Sarah.

When we brought the group back together, I called on Sarah, and asked her what her partner had said.

"My partner said 'low confidence,'" Sarah said.

"Tell me more about that," I encouraged.

"My partner is going through a hard time, and can't see the light at the end of the tunnel. They aren't confident in their abilities to make it through."

"What was your starting emotion?" I asked.

"Anxious," she replied.

"How did it feel to connect with another person in this way?"

"I felt seen and heard, and a little bit less alone."

"Why is that?"

"Well," Sarah said, "my partner asked really good questions."

"Tell me more about those questions," I responded.

"My partner was so good at asking these great, deep, thought-provoking questions. They created a space where I felt safe to share about my anxiety."

"It sounds like your partner is really good at listening, asking good questions, and creating a safe space. I don't want Sarah's partner to reveal themselves if they're not comfortable. But I want them to understand that Sarah is complimenting them on the things they did to make Sarah feel seen and heard."

Just then, Christina raised her hand. "That was me; I was Sarah's partner." she said.

"How does it feel to be complimented in this way?" I asked

"It feels good. I feel like my skills were validated."

"Have you ever been complimented on your question-asking skills?"

"Never."

"Did you realize that you are so good at asking questions?"

"No," she said.

"Do you think that asking good questions could be one of your superpowers?" I asked.

Christina began to cry, and then she began to explain.

The curiosity, listening ability, and empathy she had demonstrated—and that Sarah had pointed out—were actually skills that helped her get through a prior period of great adversity in her life. Sarah's compliments had reminded her of those skills, and helped reassure her that she could rely on them to overcome the new challenges she was facing.

When bad things happen in life, it's easy to feel like we don't have the ability to get through them. But Christina's curiosity, commitment to creating safe spaces for others, willingness to listen with empathy, and ability to ask deep follow-up questions were the skills she used to get through trying times. Moreover, they were the skills she used to find common ground and help others get through their struggles.

Gratitude gives us agency. Gratitude helps us realize we have the ability to get through trying times. It helps us recognize what we can offer ourselves, and other people. Because through gratitude, we shift our perspective.

When Christina went through that previous period of adversity, all she had been able to control was her curiosity, her ability to ask great questions, and to create safe spaces for others. And when she did that in her group with Sarah, they found that they had more in common than they would have ever known. They realized they belonged to each other, and to their organization.

Both of them shifted their perspectives and ended with positive emotions. And each left the experience inspired, engaged, hopeful, and optimistic—all of which would help them get through the challenges that lay ahead. *That* is a genuine sense of belonging.

# Gratitude Inquiry:

- *Reflection: Can you remember a time when you chose to blend in instead of being your truest self? How did that feel?*

- *Reflection: Like Christina, what intuitive skills have you developed over time that help you connect deeply with those around you? Empathy? Question asking? Listening with an open heart?*

- *Action: Write down the name of someone in your life who is often overlooked by the group around them. Write down 2-3 questions you could ask this person to help them feel seen and a sense of belonging.*

# We Have More in Common than You Think

*"At times, our own light goes out and is rekindled by a spark from another person. Each of us has cause to think with deep gratitude of those who have lighted the flame within us."*
– Albert Schweitzer

Gratitude helps us realize that we have more in common than we have differences.

One of the more insidious ways that stagnation takes hold of an organization is through homogeneity. When everyone has similar backgrounds, experiences, philosophies, and more, it's easy to keep people moving in the same direction. But it's disastrous for innovation. Innovation comes from bringing a diverse set of ideas to the table. And right now, businesses that can't innovate are rapidly losing ground in their industries.

Still, many of us struggle with difference. We look at people on our teams, or those we meet in the streets, and automatically assume that there is more that separates us than unites us. We see different geographical groups, religions, races, and so much more. And because we see so much difference, we assume that we won't be able to find any common ground. But that couldn't be further from the truth.

When we identify what we share, from passions to values, we can come together in meaningful ways. And to be successful in business today, we must cultivate diversity *and* recognize our similarities.

Cultivating diversity within your organization doesn't only mean hiring for a greater variety of racial and ethnic backgrounds, although that should certainly be part of your strategy. It also involves encouraging a variety of opinions to illuminate paths forward that you might not have otherwise seen.

One of the most effective ways to foster diversity of thought and the consensus necessary to make progress is by centering gratitude. As one of the most universal constants across cultures and languages, gratitude provides a bridge for growth and appreciation between different viewpoints.

A University of Central Florida study demonstrated the impact of implementing a simple gratitude ritual at the office. Researchers instructed participants to write about what they were grateful for at work and found that the intervention significantly improved workplace culture. Employees in the gratitude condition reported greater self-control and, according to their colleagues, subsequently engaged in less rudeness, gossip, and ostracism.

Why does gratitude work so well?

It strengthens the bond between participants, framing differences as something to be celebrated and explored. Any walls of negativity that were once up, fall down.

The first step in using gratitude to unite your organization? Acknowledge the gratitude everyone shares. For example, our team is spread out across different time zones, countries, and continents. A common point of connection is our ability to be grateful to others, regardless of the situation—good or bad.

We've spent time cultivating gratitude in our culture, and it's never been more beneficial. Gratitude helps us connect to people from different backgrounds because it is a universal human trait, feeling, and behavior. When our diverse team comes together to express who or what they are grateful for, they're better able to empathize with those from different upbringings and backgrounds. They see value in what they each bring to the table. And they're better equipped to put their individual strengths—and those of their colleagues—to work.

## Gratitude Inquiry:

- *Reflection: What qualities did you originally judge in others that were different, that ended up being the best part about them?*

- *Reflection: What are some perceived differences that you see between you and your coworkers? What can you learn from these differences?*

- *Action: Reach out to one person on your team that you don't have much in common with and tell them what you've learned from them that's had a positive impact.*

# Addressing the Empathy Deficit

*"Showing gratitude is one of the simplest yet
most powerful things humans can do for each other."*
– Randy Pausch

Why is it so hard to recognize common ground? People have a habit of focusing on what's going wrong, rather than what's going right. We have a habit of judging those that we perceive to be different, rather than celebrating all that we share.

Much of the time, feeling like we have more differences than similarities with another person can be chalked up to a lack of empathy. Roman Krznaric, author of *Empathy: What It Is and Why It Matters*, defines empathy as "the art of imaginatively stepping into the shoes of another person, understanding their feelings and perspectives, and using that knowledge to guide your action." You've got to learn to live with the brothers and sisters around you, as humans have been doing for hundreds of thousands of years, by understanding what life is like for them.

But in this day and age, that's proven to be a particular challenge. In their article titled, "The U.S. Has an Empathy Deficit," Judith Hall and Mark Leary explain that, "whenever people are troubled or hurting or dealing with serious problems, they want to feel that other people understand what they are going through and are concerned. But opportunities to give and receive empathy feel less than adequate these days: decreased social interaction, online get-togethers, air hugs and masked conversations are not quite up to the task—and people are often so preoccupied with their own struggles that they aren't as attuned to other people's problems as they otherwise might be."

When you lack empathy for those around you, members of your community seem more like objects than people with heartbeats—ones that sound a whole lot like yours. And that lack of empathy often comes from the subconscious struggles we have with ourselves.

Picture someone with whom you think you're in conflict. You may very well be in conflict with them because they just happen to be there. You may be in conflict with them because it's easier than being in conflict with yourself. And you're probably not showing them any empathy at all.

If you want to step back and take a look at the conflict in your life, you must ask yourself, *Is this conflict a product of my own doing, or is it truly based on others' behaviors?*

See, when negative situations occur in life, we often respond with anger, shame, judgment, and mistrust. They can cloud our vision, making our peers seem like enemies. But the conflict we sense is often just *our* reactions to the situation at hand. We have to own them, rather than projecting them on others. We must seek to empathize with the people around us.

My friend Monica is a Diversity, Equity, and Inclusion (DEI) leader. Monica frequently creates policies that enable people to connect by honoring their differences. To do that effectively, she helps people ask and answer the question, *Is the person I'm interacting with trying to hurt me? Or do they actually mean well?*

Most of the time, when a negative interaction occurs, we assume the perceived perpetrator is out to get us. When we do that, we tend to cement in our mind that the whole *world* is out to get us. You can see how quickly such considerations can send us spiraling into an unproductive place.

How do we avoid this thought pattern? We can start by asking the person with whom we're in conflict about their true intention.

We can also ask ourselves some questions about the other person and their intentions:

What's going on in their lives that could make them react in such a way?

Could that moment have arisen by accident?

If they didn't mean us any harm, we can work through the issue.

*The Anatomy of Peace* follows the true-life story of a Jewish man and an Arab man who came together against all odds. Each of their fathers had been killed by the other's ethnic cousins. How did they learn to forgive each other, and find a deeper connection along the way?

They surmised that, to see the change we want to see in others, we must first make it in ourselves. We must clean our side of the street before pointing at the trash on other side. That begins with taking a step back to ponder, reflect, and ask ourselves—and them—about the true intention behind the troubling interaction.

When we learn to see the world through others' eyes, we grow our capacity to empathize with them. And we can use gratitude to do it. We canur Signature Gratitude Question to ask those with whom we are in conflict about the stories in their life. That gives us the power of perspective.

In short, if we change the way we view the world, we change the way the world reacts to us.

## Gratitude Inquiry:

- *Reflection: As Monica would ask, when negative interactions or situations occur, are you someone who assumes the world is out to get you? Or do you give people the benefit of the doubt?*

- *Reflection: When was the last time someone showed you genuine empathy and how did that impact you or make you feel?*

- *Action: Like the true story of a Jewish man and an Arab man, picture someone with whom you think you're in conflict. Is this conflict a product of my own doing, or is it truly based on someone telling me I need to be in conflict with that person (because of team dynamics, cultural difference, parental guidance, etc.)?*

# Finding Belonging
# Amidst Our Differences

*"Those who have a strong sense of love*
*and belonging have the courage to be imperfect."*
– Brene Brown

One day, my friends Lori Cornmesser and Cedric Griffin called with an interesting request.

"Chris," Lori said, "I'd like to bring you in to facilitate an event. Can you host a Virtual Gratitude Experience™ with a group of my Black friends and colleagues."

"Thank you so much for thinking of me," I told her, "But do you think I'm the right person to facilitate a safe space for that group?" We were in the middle of 2020. George Floyd had just been murdered, and conversations about race were flooding our airwaves, social media channels, and interpersonal conversations. I was quite aware of the fact that I was a white guy living in the bubble of New York City.

"You're an expert at facilitating safe spaces. Your background doesn't matter. You're there to listen, empathize, and ask good questions."

I agreed to give it a try.

When I facilitated that Virtual Gratitude Experience™, I took on a posture of otherness. I thought about who I was serving first and foremost, and I came in to be a question-asker and—more importantly—a listener. Because of the way I approached the group, giving every member the space to be their full selves, they felt comfortable to share.

The experience served as a powerful opportunity for the participants to identify all the good in their lives, de-stress, and shift their mood—especially during a period that felt so fraught with tension.

After the session, Lori called me again. "I think we are missing a huge opportunity here," she said.

"What's that?" I asked.

"The opportunity to serve the DEIB space: Diversity, Equity, Inclusion, and Belonging. Why don't we go into companies and help them bring diverse groups of individuals together through gratitude? They can find connection by giving gratitude for their differences." She explained that belonging doesn't come from finding people with the exact same experiences and beliefs that you have. **True belonging comes when you can show up exactly as you are—when you don't have to change who you are to be seen and heard.**

"Diversity is no longer a nice-to-have; it's a need-to-have," Lori explained. "Bringing people together from all walks of life is the only way to build a rich and stimulating environment where both conventional and unconventional ideas can flourish. We are investing in diversity and inclusion and leveraging our team's curiosity, energy, background and capabilities to build something big together. Diversity helps us understand our customers better. And in a sense, even the adversaries."

After I got off the phone with Lori, I called my friend Court Roberts. Court is an experience designer in the DEI space, and together, we built out a year long, multi-part series on belonging.

We began by inviting different Employee Resource Groups (ERGs) to come together: LGBT groups, meeting neurodivergent groups, meeting Black groups, meeting women's groups. Then, our sessions expanded to the rest of the organization. Eventually, what started off as a DEI program morphed into company-wide leadership and belonging programs.

With each session we got deeper. First, we helped teams and organizations connect through our Signature Gratitude Question, inviting them to give gratitude to someone they hadn't thought to thank.

After we established a baseline of appreciation and connection, we had them reflect on the tough stuff. At one of our experiences, we posed the question, "What's one moment of adversity that you've overcome in your life or career that none of your friends or colleagues know about?" and asked them to share in breakout groups.

Once again, they found common ground—this time amidst adversity. It was proof that one thing we all have in common is suffering. Another person's trauma or adversity may look differently than ours, but the underlying emotions are similar. And when we can show up as who we are, *and* identify the things we share, we can create an environment where everyone feels they can bring their whole selves to the table.

The effects of these sessions remained long after the experiences wrapped.

## Gratitude Inquiry:

- *Reflection: What types of diversity are present in the friendships and relationships in your life? Where in your life are you saying no to more diverse friendships?*

- *Reflection: Think back to an occasion when you've felt safe and accepted in a group of people unlike yourself - what elements were present? What made it a safe space for you?*

- *Action: Reach out to the Lori's in your life that inspire you to find true belonging amongst your differences and thank them for inspiring moral courage in your life.*

# Mudita:
# The Antidote to Envy



*"Envy is the art of counting the
other fellow's blessings instead of your own."*
– Harold Coffin

You've probably heard the old adage, "Comparison is the thief of joy." It's true: comparison robs us of contentment. When we measure our success against the accomplishments or acquisitions of others, we become envious—resentful about all the good in their lives. That makes us miserable, plagued by self-hatred and isolation.

We become convinced that others have received far greater blessings than we have, and that means there's something wrong with us. As a result, we find ourselves building false hierarchies. We are envious of someone else, and imagine that means they are better than us. Or, we believe we are being envied by others, because we are better than them. That constant comparison makes us pretty lonely.

Socrates said "envy is the ulcer of the soul," meaning that by spending too much time worrying about what others have and don't have, we do slow and steady damage to ourselves.

Moreover, envy is very hard to talk about with others. How on earth can you go up to a friend and tell them you're envious of their life? That would only make you feel the pain of "lack" more keenly—and likely make them pretty uncomfortable.

Plus, in a world dominated by social media, we convince ourselves that we should only share the perfect moments and shroud the setbacks from view. As a result, we compare ourselves to others' highlight reels, and sow the seeds of envy all along. But the truth is that the envy spurred by social media is based on falsehoods.

On social media, we see the perfectly filtered lives that our friends and icons promote. Meanwhile, we tend to focus on the not-so-nice looking parts of ourselves. We compare our worst moments to the peak experiences our friends are touting. Social media tricks us into thinking that we are connecting with others when we post and consume content, but in reality, we're only comparing ourselves to them.

But, according to a research article by Smith, Turner, Leach, and Weston, grateful people are less likely to feel envy or resentment.

Why?

When you focus on others' benevolence—which gratitude builds—"you are less likely to engage in jealousy and resentment, as a grateful person appreciates the positive qualities in others and can feel happy over the good fortune that happens to others."

In his article for *Greater Good Magazine*, Dr. Robert Emmons, one of the world's leading scientific experts on gratitude, describes gratitude as the antidote to envy: "You can't feel envious and grateful at the same time. They're incompatible feelings, because if you're grateful, you can't resent someone for owning things you don't."

Gratitude illuminates the good and giving nature of others, while envy only highlights perceived competitors' superiority and one's own isolation. A deeply grateful person focuses more on what's going right in their life, rather than trying to fix what they perceive to be going wrong (we'll touch on this in a few sections). A grateful person will find themselves burdened by the misery of envy less often, and will be quick to find value in their own abilities and endowments. A grateful person will understand that they belong, that they are valued authentically by others—just for being themselves. It reinforces that we are enough.

Rather than being envious of what you don't have, try celebrating the success of others and you too will ride the tide toward a healthier, happier outlook. In Pali, an ancient Indian language, this concept is called *mudita*, which means "to delight in the good fortunes or the accomplishments of others." In essence, it's the opposite of envy.

When you see someone show pride in their achievements on social media, click that share button and tell your community about what they've accomplished. When you do, you'll become a foot soldier in *their* movement.

When we celebrate the successes of others, we also encourage them to celebrate *our* journey and help us along the way. That drives connection—yet another thing to be grateful for.

# Gratitude Inquiry:

- *Reflection: What are areas of your life where you only share the highlight reel? Could it be possible others are doing the same?*

- *Reflection: When was the last time you felt jealous or envious of another person? What are you choosing to believe about them or their situation?*

- *Action: Choose someone's success around you today and share their accomplishment with your community on social media or in a small group setting. Observe how it makes you feel.*

# Using Gratitude to Heal Broken Relationships

*"A noble person is mindful and thankful
of the favors he receives from others."*
– Buddha

n 2019, my team and I made frequent trips to Los Angeles to produce a series of in-person Gratitude Dinners. We would fly into town to produce these experiences in partnership with our dear friends Zach Zelner, Ali Mirza, Cam Fordham, and Taylor Ciallella. Our goals were always to bring together a great group of founders, CEOs, artists, and entertainment folks and help them find meaningful connection through gratitude. These attendees hailed from a variety of industries, from media, to entertainment, tech, real estate, and beyond.

Before moving to our home at the AKA West Hollywood, we would always rent an AirBnB—singer Tom Jones's home, way up in the hills of Bel Air—and host our dinners there. With the location squared away, Zach and I would often talk about the guest list. One time, he asked if one of his business co-founders, Todd, could come to dinner.

I was surprised by the question. Over the past several months, they hadn't talked much. The two had built a successful e-commerce company in the pet industry together, growing it from zero to $40 million in sales in the first eighteen months. As fast as that company grew, and as tumultuous as that growth was, Todd and Zach eventually had a falling out. They disagreed on fundamental terms of the business. They accused each other of different things, and the relationship soured from there.

Nonetheless, Zach came to me that afternoon and asked if it was alright if Todd came to dinner.

"Of course," I said, "that would be great." It would be the first time they had seen each other in many months.

Well, among the crowd of eighteen founders and CEOs were Zach and Todd. They sat across the table from each other. When we arrived at the appropriate part of the evening, I asked our Signature Gratitude Question: "If you could give credit or thanks to one person in your life, someone you don't thank enough, who would that be?"

Per usual, people shared a beautiful variety of answers. Some talked about their mother, or their father, or their third grade teacher, or that bad ex-boss, or ex-girlfriend. Then, Zach stood up and gave credit thanks to his co-founder, Todd, who—of course—was there in the room.

He talked about the long nights, the hard conversations, the difficult choices that they had made through the years, and how silly it was that their relationship had become so turbulent. And as Zach gave gratitude to Todd, tears welled up in both of their eyes. When Zach was done, he walked around the table and gave Todd a hug.

It was an incredible moment that touched everyone in attendance—I don't think there was a single dry eye in the house. And that simple act of gratitude kept working its magic. It healed their relationship. They've since worked through their challenges and made amends.

Their business is feeling the effects of Zach's words too. Now, neither one of them takes a work trip without the other. In fact, they just broke ground on a massive warehouse in Atlanta, Georgia, and hired hundreds more employees to staff it.

It's a true testament to the power of gratitude, and the ways in which it can remind us that we belong to each other.

## Gratitude Inquiry:

- *Reflection: What are some past examples of repaired relationships in your life? What were the steps that led to the repair?*

- *Reflection: Who are you currently in a perceived conflict with? What have you missed out on in life because of that conflict?*

- *Action: Reach out to one person you're in conflict with this week and express gratitude without having the pressure of receiving thanks in return.*

# Making Enemies into Friends



Gratitude not only heals broken relationships, it can also build positive connections in places they've never been.

Do you have an enemy—big or small? It may be a colleague at work with whom you always seem to butt heads, a family member that never sees your side of things, or an acquaintance with wildly different political beliefs.

*The Anatomy of Peace* highlights the value of overcoming differences to forge new bonds. The book has been a best-selling conflict resolution tool for years.

The story begins with six sets of parents dropping their kids off at a wilderness rehab facility in the desert of Arizona—one very similar to the wilderness treatment facility my parents sent me to as a twenty-year-old kid. The facility is run by two men, one Arab and one Jewish. Both are from the Middle East, and both men's fathers were killed by the other's tribe.

The parents figure that if the owners, an Arab and a Jewish person, can have a successful rehab facility together, they must know something about conflict resolution.

As part of the program, the parents have agreed to spend two days in Arizona as well. They believe that they'll be learning how the program will transform their children. But they soon find out that those next two days will be spent understanding how *they* must make adjustments to realize the change they'd like to see. They will be learning their part in their kids' behavior.

Along the way, they come to see that, to get someone across the table to see your side of things, you must first empathize with them and their perspective. You must learn about where they're coming from and see them as a full-fledged person—not just your opposition. When you stop seeing the person across the fence as an object, and start seeing them as a human being, you can build bonds you never thought possible.

How do we do that?

We could wish, want, and wait for the other to change first. But the truth is, that will never happen.

When we have a fundamental divide, neither of the parties will give up any ground. As a result, a conflict continues for an extended period of time unchecked. If you are going to effectively engage with someone who has a different set of opinions, something must change—and that something is likely you.

Now, that doesn't mean you have to throw everything you believe out the window. Rather, it could be as simple as a slight shift in perspective. Let's take a look at the Arbinger Institute's Influence Pyramid.

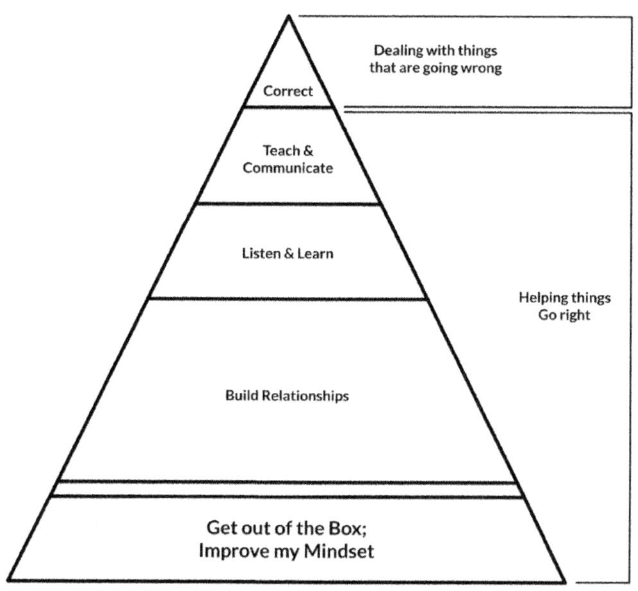


To improve our mindsets and influence effectively, we must spend most of our time helping things go right: building relationships, listening and learning from others, and teaching and communicating what we've learned. Meanwhile, we should be spending the least amount of time dealing with what's going wrong, and doing so by correcting others.

But the unfortunate reality is that our society has flipped the script on this pyramid. Most of us spend 90 percent of our time dealing with things that are going wrong, instead of helping things go right. We forget to appreciate the good, and only see the bad. It's the exact mindset that almost caused my demise. That is the plague of ingratitude.

We try fixing others—whether it be our children, spouses, or employees—by disciplining them for not acting as we'd like.

We've got to flip our societal model on its head so it looks more like this one. To become agents of change, we have to spend most of our time helping and appreciating things going right, rather than simply correcting what's gone wrong. We need to put our energy into building relationships, listening, learning, and—to a lesser extent—teaching.

How does this relate to gratitude? Gratitude helps us shift our perspective. Instead of dwelling on the negative, gratitude helps us appreciate the good. Leading up to my NSSI episode in late 2021, there were so many things going right in my life. But all I could focus on was fixing the small number of things going wrong. Gratitude helps us acknowledge the moral courage and wisdom necessary to be the change we seek, to flip that script on appreciation. Gratitude is the micro-intervention that helps spark a new way of thinking about the moments around us.

You can probably guess what I'm going to suggest. Try approaching that enemy with gratitude. Communicate one benefit you've received from them or from your conflict over time. When something is troubling us in this life—an injustice, a broken relationship, or unmet expectations—we can learn to give gratitude to those experiences, appreciating the positive benefits they've created in our life and the resilience they've helped us develop.

What are the perceived benefits that have arisen as a result of that conflict? That's where we can begin to turn the tide.

# Gratitude Inquiry:

- *Reflection: Take a look at the Arbinger Institute pyramid again. Do you spend more of your time dealing with things that are going wrong, or investing time in helping things go right?*

- *Reflection: Where in your life are you relying on others to change when the true change starts with yourself?*

- *Action: Make a fearless and searching moral inventory of those you've wronged in life - was the conflict actually a result of your own doing?*

# PART III

# The Case for Gratitude in Tough Times

*"If you are distressed by anything external, the
pain is not due to the thing itself, but to your estimate of it;
and this you have the power to revoke at any moment."*
– Marcus Aurelius

# A Note on Trauma

We can't talk about tough times without referencing trauma.

Not everyone's past is full of happy memories. When you're making space for gratitude that is rooted in a specific, personal experience, you have to understand and make room for trauma too.

Abuse, neglect, sudden separation, living with someone struggling with mental health or substance use disorders—these experiences can all have lasting effects. Trauma disrupts well-being. It can wreak mental, physical, social, and emotional havoc, and last long after the situation resolves.

Trauma can also be multigenerational or community-wide. Poverty, racism, discrimination, oppression, gun violence, war—these experiences can all come into play when you dive deep with gratitude. That means when you ask someone else about for whom or what they are grateful, you must be ready to get into the trauma too—or to recognize its effects.

It's also important to note that what is traumatic to someone else may not be traumatic to you. If it's trauma to them, it's trauma. Don't ever compare your trauma to theirs—and vice versa. That plays into the entitlement issues we discussed previously.

Responses to similar traumas can also be completely different. As we dig into our own trauma and that of others, let's remember not to judge others' responses. When something horrible happens to us, we are forever changed. Even if we never talk about that event again, the effects stay with us. Let's respect what we've each been through, and help each other move forward.

# Post-Traumatic Growth

*"It is not a person or situation that affects your life;
it is the meaning you give to that person or situation,
which influences your emotions and actions. Your choice
is to change the meaning you give it or change your
response, in order to create the outcome you want."*
– Shannon L. Alder

It's easy to be grateful when things are going well. But the thing about life is that it's not just filled with positive moments; life is also filled with really shitty ones.

Anyone who's been on Earth for some period of time knows that shit happens, but therein lies the opportunity!

Our dear friend and partner Ryan Serhant once said to us, "It is my belief that from crisis comes opportunity and from endurance comes a path forward. In order to find opportunity in crises, we have to look at the lessons learned from our past."

Humans have been surviving hard times since our inception. In fact, prior to the eighteenth century, most people accepted suffering as the norm. It's what you do with it that counts.

Many wise people, across multiple traditions, have taught that suffering brings clarity and illumination. For Buddha, suffering was the first rule of life. Nietzsche wrote that "to live is to suffer; to survive is to make sense of the suffering." Helen Keller said "character cannot be developed in ease and quiet. Only through experience of trial and suffering can the soul be strengthened, ambition inspired, and success achieved."

Somewhere along the way to the present day, the way we thought about the world began to shift. In many places, catastrophes and crises grew fewer and farther in between and creature comforts like electricity and running water became the norm, which meant that people worried less about surviving and more about living well. The problem is that suffering still exists—we just avoid talking about it.

The writer Glennon Doyle articulates avoidance as her personal failing, but ultimately describes a cultural phenomenon based on bad advice. In *Untamed*, she writes "I did not know that I was supposed to feel everything. I thought I was supposed to feel happy. I thought that happy was for feeling and that pain was for fixing and numbing and deflecting and hiding and ignoring."

According to psychologist Matthew Tull, "avoidance refers to any action designed to prevent the occurrence of an uncomfortable emotion such as fear, sadness, or shame. For example, a person may try to avoid difficult emotions through the use of substances or dissociation," or through procrastination or shutting others out.

But that avoidance often backfires. Denying painful and negative emotions can lead to feeling those emotions more deeply and for longer periods of time. For example, avoiding a difficult issue in a marriage might lead to resentment—which could turn to cheating, lying, and divorce. Instead of facing the facts, we avoid the painful conversations, which in turn causes more pain.

When we deny an emotion, we're actually denying our reality. This may make us feel decent in the short run, but long-term, it takes its toll. It's just not realistic to think that we can just avoid hard emotions until they go away.

Why are we avoidant in the first place? What are we afraid of?

Uncomfortable conversations. Brave conversations. Vulnerable rumblings. In *Daring Greatly*, author Brene Brown describes a rumble like this:

A rumble is a discussion, conversation, or meeting defined by a commitment to lean into vulnerability, to stay curious and generous, to stick with the messy middle of problem identification and solving, to take a break and circle back when necessary, to be fearless in owning our parts, and, as psychologist Harriet Lerner teaches, to listen with the same passion with which we want to be heard. More than anything else, when someone says, 'Let's rumble,' it cues me to show up with an open heart and mind so we can serve the work and each other, not our egos. Open hearts and open minds are critical if we want to be brave. Remember, it's not fear that gets in the way of courage – it's armor. It's the way we self-protect, shut down, and start posturing when we're in fear.

For me, the key phrase here is, "stick with the messy middle." I think that messy middle is so delicious. Rather than try to stay on the periphery of what's happening, get right in there and enjoy the passion, intimacy, and raw courage that the messy middle creates. When your heart lights up like that, so many positive outcomes occur.

That's where gratitude comes in.

In an article on his *Daily Stoic* website, Ryan Holiday surmises that "the Stoics believed that we should feel gratitude for all the people and events that form our lives. We shouldn't just be thankful for the gifts we receive, and our relationships with friends and family. We should also be aware of and grateful for the setbacks and annoyances."

Freud once said, "One day, in retrospect, the years of struggle will strike you as the most beautiful." Life itself is actually a form of suffering. To try to avoid it would be futile, so you might as well accept it, learn to cope, and even find gratitude for the challenges you'll inevitably bump up against.

Why?

Your ability to shift your perspective in the aftermath of that pain and take action in a prosocial way is what leads to a positive mental attitude. But it's not necessarily a matter of turning a negative into a positive. Others who teach gratitude will often tell you to "just think positive thoughts." Be grateful, and you'll feel happy or joyful. But the truth is, life isn't about feeling happy all the time. Sometimes, just feeling it is enough.

Mark Manson writes that one of the ways we can get through suffering is to rebrand it as sacrifice. In his book, *The Subtle Art of Not Giving A Fuck*, he explains that humans need some pain and struggle to maintain sanity and wellbeing. While too much pain will really mess us up, too little pain will make us fragile and ill-equipped for life's challenges.

But when we experience *some* pain, and we can turn it into growth, we develop resilience. We can see that pain as a tool that helps us fulfill our purpose.

Post-traumatic growth is a "theory that explains this kind of transformation following trauma. It was developed by psychologists Richard Tedeschi, PhD, and Lawrence Calhoun, PhD, in the mid-1990s, and holds that people who endure psychological struggle following adversity can often see positive growth afterward."

Tedeschi and Calhoun argue that when trauma occurs, we can respond in one of two ways. Either we can be filled with stress, anger, or depression, which turns into post-traumatic stress. Or, we can learn to find the benefits amidst our trauma and turn it into an opportunity for growth.

When post-traumatic growth occurs, people will develop new relationships, a new outlook, a new philosophy, and so much more that will lead them in a better direction.

Take, for instance, my grandfather Cristoforo Schembra, who immigrated from Sicily to the US through Ellis Island on August 2, 1916.

My grandfather went through a great deal of suffering to move his family to America. He had no money in his pocket and hardly spoke a word of English when he stowed away on a boat traveling across the Atlantic. He arrived in a country that saw him not only as the enemy (it was World War I, and he was Italian), but as an unskilled laborer only capable of bottom-of-the-barrel jobs.

He endured a lot, but he considered it all a part of his higher purpose, and that made him resilient. He would go on to open his own butcher shop, and serve his community for many years. There, he worked toward his higher purpose and helped a great deal of people through their own hard times. Decades after working alongside my grandfather, many people have said they learned the most about life while they were working alongside him.

Years later, we look back at what he did and call it sacrifice.

What do we owe the ancestors who made major sacrifices to help us live comfortably in a world that was new to them?

We owe them, and those who will come after us, our own sacrifices.

Your life won't be painless; no one's is. But what if you could take all the hard things life throws at you and find meaning in them? That's where resilience is born. And you can help birth it by remembering the sacrifices of others who helped you get where you are today. Your ability to honor those who came before you and the sacrifices they made will develop your own ability to turn the pain you're going through right now into growth and opportunity.

With that in mind, let's dive into the messy middle. In doing so, we'll realize the benefits that occur there, feel less afraid of uncertainty, strengthen relationships, improve our self-esteem and self-confidence, and learn to be productive through hard times. Sounds like it's worth the discomfort, doesn't it?

# Gratitude Inquiry:

- *Reflection: What are some avoidance techniques that you've used throughout your life to prevent feeling things like fear, sadness, or shame?*

- *Reflection: What are uncomfortable conversations that you're avoiding right now?*

- *Action: Write down in as many details as possible, the story of the sacrifice your ancestors made to get you to where you are today in life.*

# Mortality into Moral Courage and Meaning

*"Everything can be taken from a man but one thing:*
*the last of the human freedoms—to choose one's attitude in*
*any given set of circumstances, to choose one's own way."*
– Viktor Frankl

In the closing moments of writing this book, I reread Viktor Frankl's perennial bestseller, *Man's Search for Meaning*. In the book, Frankl writes that life is not about seeking pleasure, like Freud once said. It's not about seeking power, like Alfred Adler once said. Instead, life is about searching for meaning.

Frankl explains that meaning can come from working to serve others, from loving or caring for someone else, or from finding moral courage in difficult times.

My team and I don't just help people give gratitude to the positive stuff in their lives; we also help people give gratitude to the negative. We love helping people acknowledge and be grateful for the ways that they've gotten through moments of adversity, and recognize the hope, pride, optimism, and self-confidence that gives them.

In March of 2022, I found a tremendous moment of meaning in my own life. I was on the phone with my mother, and we were talking about my uncle Andrew's health, which was declining rapidly. She told me his end might be near. When I heard that, I immediately said, "Mom, I'll hop on the next flight home." I told her that I would fly in, rent a car, and drive my dad and his sister—my Godmother, Aunt Cathy—to go see my uncle in the hospital.

My mom was astounded. She couldn't believe I would drop everything to be with them, but in my mind, nothing else mattered except being there for dad. With both my parents in their seventies, I knew it was my time to step up to be there for the family.

My family has seen me at my worst. My parents, my aunt Cathy, my uncle Andrew, and cousins saw me struggle as a kid—spoiled, entitled, enabled, insecure, completely lost. I did some weird things growing up. They were there for me during that turbulent time, and this was my chance to show up for them.

The sacrifice I made to go visit, the hard conversations we navigated together, and the mature decisions we came to gave me the opportunity to be there for my family when they needed me most.

I picked up my dad and his sister in my rental car, and we drove to North Carolina to make some difficult decisions about the remainder of Uncle Andrew's life. It was tough, but it was beautiful. It made me feel grateful.

How can I be grateful for the passing of my Uncle? Not only did our time there serve as the meaningful goodbye that our family needed; it also allowed my family to see the moral courage I possess, as I step up to lead the next generation of our family.

Moral courage is the willingness to act in line with your beliefs in the face of forces that could easily lead you to behave differently. When difficult times are happening in your life, it's easy to turn away. It's easy to pretend like they're not happening. But life requires you to stand up with courage and find meaning in the ways you can and will overcome adversity.

And once you find meaning in one moment of adversity, it just gets easier. See, giving gratitude to negative experiences develops the resilience necessary to get through additional trying times. Life isn't just about picture-perfect moments and moments of pleasure. It's about finding true, meaningful connections in all seasons.

The truth is, your trauma is different from my trauma. Your suffering is different from my suffering, but we both experience pain, sadness, and triumph. When we recognize that, we can connect in powerful ways.

I encourage you to look at your life and observe the moments when you shy away from moral courage in favor of avoiding pain or even making short-term gains. When in life have you taken the easy path, instead of the one that requires a little bravery?

You'll likely notice that, while they may have saved you a little discomfort, those periods probably caused more pain in the long run.

The pleasure you seek by getting that next promotion or your next social media like will pale in comparison to the meaning you will find by stepping up and doing what's right. If you seek out those opportunities to be courageous, I can promise you a life of meaning.

Life isn't supposed to look pretty. It's filled with hard times like the one I shared. We get to choose how we respond to those events, and when we do, we'll find they deliver so much more value than we could have anticipated.

# Gratitude Inquiry:

- *Reflection: Moral courage is the willingness to act in line with your beliefs in the face of forces that could easily lead you to behave differently. When in life have you shown moral courage in the face of difficulty?*

- *Reflection: When in life have you taken the easy path, instead of the one that requires a little bravery? What was the missed opportunity?*

- *Action: Identify one person in your life who models moral courage - staying in alignment with their core values even when it requires difficult decisions. Reach out to them and let them know their courage was observed and felt.*

# Adversity into a Superpower



At some of our Virtual Gratitude Experiences™, we ask a simple question: What is one adverse experience you had that shaped you, but that none of your current colleagues or teammates know about? What's an obstacle you've had to overcome?

We then ask our attendees to respond to the prompt in writing. We set a five minute timer and encourage them to think deeply.

What was that experience?

How did you get through it?

What did that experience mean to you?

Who helped you through it?

What haven't you processed?

After the writing exercise, we break people up into groups of three and have them share these stories and insights with their colleagues.

Some talk about overcoming the doubts of others; some share about grappling with loss of loved ones; others explain how they made it through the first days, weeks, and months of debilitating injuries. Each story is raw and real and vulnerable, and each one helps people remember an important truth. When they dive back into that story, they remember that they once overcame a great period of adversity. Oftentimes, they find that the hard times they are going through now pale in comparison to what they have already been through.

From there, we reconvene and debrief, giving people the opportunity to share with the group as a whole. Some people share how good it feels to hear other people's stories of adversity, and some people describe how good it felt to share their own.

We then ask them to ponder another set of questions:

What new superpowers have you developed because of your story?

How has what you experienced in the past equipped you to meet the challenges of the future?

How will you use your superpowers to support your team?

This step is important because it helps them realize that a negative past experience equips them with certain benefits. They get the opportunity to not only recognize the superpower they have developed, but also to think about how those superpowers improve their lives on a consistent basis. After they reflect on their superpowers for a few minutes, we have them write down a statement:

I'm excited to contribute my superpowers of __________
to our team, and I'm going to start by __________ .

We then ask them to drop their sentence into the group chat. When they do, they actually find a tremendous amount of similarities between the sentences they share and those of their teammates.

At one experience we produced, I met a young woman named Vasanti. I asked her to tell us her story of overcoming adversity, and how it turned into her superpower.

Vasanti shared a story about growing up in India. "If you grew up in India, and you wanted to leave the country, everyone would tell you that you need to get really good at computer programming, and get a coding job in America," she explained. So, Vasanti enrolled in a program to become a coder. But she wasn't the best coder in school. One teacher even bullied her for her limited skills in front of her peers.

Her teacher's words embarrassed her, as they would many of us. Worse: they made her feel that she'd never succeed, no matter how hard she tried. Vasanti was discouraged. She was ready to change her career path altogether. But she decided to give herself one more chance and teach herself to code.

She found that she was great at teaching herself, and became so good that she not only learned to code, she overcame the expectations of others. Eventually, she found a computer programming job in the United States.

"Vasanti, it sounds like you like rising up to meet challenges," I told her

She teared up. After a moment, she said, "You're right. I do. I love being told I can't do something now, just so I can rise up to the challenge and prove others wrong."

"It sounds like you're a good self-starter. It sounds like you're a lifelong learner," I said.

Her eyes welled up again. "Yes. I love figuring out ways I can succeed."

I looked around the room and I saw a lot of people nodding their heads and writing things down on paper.

"Vasanti, look around. I think a lot of people love this value of yours." Ryan, one of her teammates, was writing too. "Ryan, what are you jotting down right now?" I asked him.

"Honestly? I'm listing out new assignments that I can give to Vasanti."

"Vasanti, does it make you happy to know that people are already thinking of new challenges that you can help them overcome?"

She nodded, and I could see how proud she was.

Vasanti's story demonstrates that we can acknowledge past moments of adversity and turn them into our strengths. The bullying she experienced helped her become a self-starter who rises up to meet challenges. And those experiences and skills benefit her team, as she continues to promote creativity, innovation, and growth for herself and among her peers.

Further, by sharing what she had been through and what it had taught her about herself and her skill-set, she empowered her team to reach out to her when they encountered a problem or challenge.

Recognizing and sharing the tough stuff helps teams grow their understanding of one another, build trust, and get closer. It's just one way that we can transform adversity into a superpower.

# Gratitude Inquiry:

- *Reflection: What's one moment of adversity you've overcome, but many of your colleagues don't know about?What was that experience? How did you get through it? What did that experience mean to you? Who helped you through it? What haven't you processed?*

- *Reflection: What superpower have you developed as a result of that adversity?*

- *Action: Write down the story and superpowers you reflected on above and share that story with someone this week. Finish the story by saying ". . . and I'm so grateful this occurred in my life."*

# Hurt into Healing

*"My barn having burned down, I can now see the moon."*
– Mizuta Masahide

When you attend one of our Virtual Gratitude Experiences™, or take some time to answer our Signature Gratitude Question, some of what you uncover when you dive deep into your past won't be very positive. Difficult memories may appear like dark holes, unprocessed and heavy with emotion.

When those memories come up, don't run from them. Instead, aim to process, and then give gratitude to them. That will help you build resilience.

I can't remember fifteen years of my life. Yes, you read that correctly. Ages five to twenty are a big ol' blur. When I was just a kindergartner, a doctor put me on very high doses of Adderall and all sorts of other drugs to combat my ADHD. That led to confusion, memory loss, and difficulty relating to my peers.

For a long time, I blamed myself. *How could I be born so different that I needed pills to fit in? What was so wrong with me that I needed to be heavily medicated just to socialize?* My perceived problems showed up in every aspect of my life, affecting the way I made friends, made money, and viewed my future at large.

After a while—and multiple stints in rehab—I stopped blaming myself, and started to transfer blame to the doctor who gave me those pills and made me feel like a monster for taking them. That filled me up with rage, anger, shame, and resentment. *I mean, who was he for giving me this diagnosis? How did he know what was best for me? Because of him, my childhood is a gosh darn black hole.*

But over time, I learned to thank that doctor.

I would never wish a fifteen-year memory gap on anyone, but this particular negative experience led me down a non-linear path of discovering my passion for human connection. It led me to drop out of college, ship off to rehab, live on a glacier in Patagonia, become a boat captain, start a few companies, and move to New York City. None of that would have happened if I had taken a predictable, linear path.

Of course, there's a downside to the twists and turns I've taken myself down over the years: it's been a lonely road. Along the way though, I went from just reliving those memories, to finding the benefits they offer. And because I know what it feels like to be an outsider, I now facilitate experiences in which everyone gets to belong. On a daily basis, I get to share my story—including my grief surrounding those missing fifteen years. That helps me continue to process it and extract even more benefits.

The trauma I was put through has actually turned into the greatest medicine of all. Earlier, we talked about how practicing gratitude releases dopamine in the brain. That dopamine inspires laser-like focus. Now, I don't have to take ADHD medicine to accomplish great things in life; I can rely on my gratitude practice to guide me. Using gratitude to help me achieve laser-like focus—the flow state we were writing about in previous sections. Teaching gratitude has given me a life of meaning, one I likely never would have found if it weren't for my non-linear path and the immense challenges I encountered along the way.

When we recognize the positive outcomes that came from our negative memories, we change the narrative. We allow ourselves to heal our deepest wounds.

## Gratitude Inquiry:

- *Reflection: Similar to my story of being heavily medicated at a young age, have you ever experienced being an outsider? What was it about you or your personality that felt different than the norm?*

- *Reflection: Do you have any friends or coworkers who might feel left out because they are outside of the "group norm"? How have their differences positively contributed to your life?*

- *Action: Write down one part of your personality (like my ADHD) that people said would always hold you back, but has become your strongest character strength.*

# Negative Experiences into Resilience

*"Everyone here has the sense that
right now is one of those moments
when we are influencing the future."*
– Steve Jobs

"Resilience" is trending, and for good reason. Our world seems to be in constant flux, and everybody is talking about how we need to develop the skills to adapt. Without resilience, every lost opportunity feels like a catastrophe. Failure and setbacks can feel like points of no return despite being normal—if unpleasant—aspects of life.

I personally think resilience is sexy. I'd rather be complimented on my resilience in the face of adversity, than on some unique talent or physical trait.

However, resilience isn't something that you can develop just by reading a book or watching a tv show. It's a muscle, and gratitude can help you build it.

Dr. Christian Gloria and Dr. Mary Steinhardt explain that "gratitude fosters adaptive coping mechanisms. By managing positive emotions like satisfaction, happiness, and pleasure;

gratitude enhances our emotional resilience and builds our inner strength to combat stress." These coping mechanisms help us bounce back from difficult events.

One of the key ways to develop resilience is through a gratitude practice. Practicing gratitude rewires our brain to be more positive and resilient. Being grateful activates your hypothalamus, the area of the brain associated with energy maintenance and stress control, reducing your susceptibility to anxiety and helping you muster the motivation to get through tough times. It physically changes the brain to better handle adversity.

What separates people who thrive in stressful times from those who break down when faced with adversity?

Research by Dr. Michele M. Tugade suggests that resilient people experience positive emotions more frequently.

Gratitude reminds you that we'll get through this, too. It can be difficult to be grateful for negative experiences, but by shifting your focus to the positive outcomes of these experiences, you take power away from the bad and put it in the hands of the good. Doing so helps you see that you're able to weather any storm that comes your way.

Researchers McCullough and Witvliet say that gratitude builds emotional resilience by:

- Helping us to see the positive things in life
- Fighting the negative ruminations and rebuilding pessimistic thoughts with optimistic ones
- Staying grounded and accepting the present situation, even if that is a harsh reality
- Identifying and focusing only on solutions

- Maintaining good health by regulating our metabolic functioning and by controlling the hormonal imbalances
- Sustaining relationships and appreciating people who are there for us. As a result, we feel more loved, cared for, and more hopeful

Think about a time where the world has presented you with an almost insurmountable obstacle, which you somehow overcame. While we cannot ignore the fact that the struggle occurred, we can give gratitude to the way we overcame it and what we learned along the way. Giving gratitude to how we face adversity is how we develop emotional resilience.

Unemployed, relying on another person's support while trying to figure out what you're going to do with your life, feeling directionless or unsure, does any of that sound familiar?

Most of us can relate to this predicament in one way or another. At the beginning of the COVID pandemic, unemployment rates ramped up to 16 percent in America. That is over 45 million people in the United States alone.

Although situations like the one so many of us found ourselves facing aren't ideal, they're a part of life—and almost all of us face them at one point or another. Whether you lose your job due to unforeseen circumstances or you quit your dayjob to pursue a greater purpose, these low points in life need to be celebrated, not hidden away.

Why?

They inevitably make us stronger.

Take for instance, David Paynter's story of resilience. David had a good job, with a decent salary and a company car. And then he decided to leave his job and use his life savings to start a business. He became solely dependent on his wife's salary, a big leap of faith considering they had two young children to support.

As he invested early mornings, late nights, and all that unearned income into his dream, people around him were telling him that the idea he loved and put his life savings into probably wouldn't pan out. Although it hurt not to have their buy-in, he never doubted his decision to pursue his dream.

That didn't mean David didn't suffer; he endured countless sleepless nights. He worried that things wouldn't work. And the stress lasted for over a year, until his new business took off. It was the most challenging year of his life. But it was also the greatest year he'd ever had. Do you know why?

It brought out the best in David. It made him into the person and businessman he is today. David is more resilient and grateful than ever because of that dark year. And instead of filing that year away in the deep recesses of his brain, David reflects on that time often. He gives gratitude to those tough times, and the ways he overcame.

Not only does David give gratitude to those times, but he also shares his story with others. Sharing moments of vulnerability builds connection and creates inspiration. That year wasn't just a part of David's story; it marked a turning point in his life. The leap of faith he took to build his business paid off—but it was only after all the hard work that he got to reap any of the benefits.

It's okay to be afraid to take that next step. It's okay if it doesn't work out right away. It's okay to struggle. Gratitude can help us find the value in our pain and understand its greater purpose in our lives. So take that leap of faith and know that it may hurt, but that finding value in—and being grateful for—that discomfort will make you more resilient. And it's resilience that determines success, far more than a person's education, training, or experience. That's certainly something to be grateful for.

## Gratitude Inquiry:

- *Reflection: Think about people in your life who thrive in stressful times. Now, reflect on people in your life who break down when faced with adversity? What are the differences in their two approaches?*

- *Reflection: What is an experience where your resilience, rather than innate talent, is what helped you overcome an insurmountable obstacle?*

- *Action: Write about the five character strengths you possess that allowed you to be resilient during your great time of need.*

# Unpleasant Events into Positive Outcomes

*"It's your reaction to adversity, not adversity itself
that determines how your life's story will develop."*
– Dieter F. Uchtdorf

Philip Watkins coined the term "grateful processing." His hypothesis is that when you don't just recall a negative memory, but also feel grateful for it and find the benefits it has imparted, you give yourself the gift of closure. To do that, we can turn to grateful processing: identifying the positive outcomes of unpleasant events.

Daniel Miller explains that grateful processing helps us create a serene state of mind by:

- Redirecting our focus from what is troubling or worrying us to what lifts our spirit—from the negative to the positive
- Helping us realize what's actually at stake, and adjust accordingly
- Reducing fear, and the anxiety that comes with it
- Enabling us to let go of our desire for control, and thus creating space for serenity

Grateful processing might involve seeing how a troubling event in your life helped you develop a superpower that has allowed you to flourish in a way you never expected.

Phillip Watkins, and his team proposed that:

"Grateful processing of unpleasant, agitated, open memories helps bring closure to recollections. Thinking about how one can be grateful for the consequences of a difficult experience might give the event some purpose, and therefore bring closure to the memory. By identifying positive consequences of a stressful event that one can be grateful for, this should help the memory fit more coherently into one's good life story."

To test his theory that giving gratitude to unpleasant, unprocessed experiences could help subjective well-being, Watkins and his team conducted a writing experiment, assigning 128 participants to one of three different groups:

1. A control condition in which participants wrote about things unrelated to the open, negative memory.
2. An emotional control condition, in which the participants wrote freely about the negative memory, just recalling whatever came up.
3. A gratitude condition, in which people wrote about the positive outcomes of the open memory.

The emotional control and gratitude groups were told to think about an open memory that is troubling from their past, that they had yet to process—something that intrudes on their consciousness from time to time, that feels like unfinished business.

Watkins then asked the gratitude condition participants to ponder a set of questions surrounding their negative experience:

1. As a result of this event, what kinds of things do you now feel thankful or grateful for?
2. How has this event benefited you as a person?
3. How have you grown?
4. Were there personal strengths that grew out of your experience?
5. How has the event made you better able to meet the challenges of the future?
6. How has the event put your life into perspective?
7. How has this event helped you appreciate the truly important people and things in your life?
8. In sum, how can you be thankful for the beneficial consequences that have resulted from this event?

The results were remarkable! While those in the emotional control group received some benefits from writing about their experience, those in the gratitude condition experienced more closure than all the other conditions tested.

Processing negative experiences helps us let them go. We know that, due to negative memory bias, we're more likely to notice when bad things happen to us. Studies show that ruminating on negative thoughts and events—repeatedly turning them over in your mind—can lead to depression. Talking through these thoughts with a therapist or writing them down can help. When you make a concerted effort to get them out of your head, you trigger neutral analysis, and eventually, resolution.

Writing down or talking through our stories requires organizing, integrating, and analyzing our problems with a focus on solution-generation, or—at least—acceptance. When we process stories about our traumatic experiences, we can better understand our emotions.

Other researchers have observed the benefits of grateful processing. Dru Masingale found that "grateful college students had roughly half of the posttraumatic symptoms as less grateful students after a stressful event." Researcher Todd Kashdan and his team found the same phenomenon among a group of Vietnam veterans, and others have found similar results among students coping with the impact of September 11.

Grateful processing is powerful when it comes to long-term well-being too. Instead of providing a momentary mood boost, it's reframing skill that lasts long after the intervention itself. That means that the effects of our sixty- or ninety-minute sessions last far longer than the events themselves.

## Gratitude Inquiry:

- *Reflection: What negative memories or thoughts do you spend time ruminating on?*

- *Reflection: Who do you know that took the time to do the work to resolve past trauma and find gratitude for that situation? How has their life shifted as a result?*

- *Action: Write about the positive outcomes of two unpleasant, agitating, or open memories from your past.*

# Struggles into Benefits



*"There's no education like adversity."*
– Disraeli

What do you do when you're in the midst of a difficult situation? I know how much of a struggle it can be. You may be staring down a crisis and wondering how you'll ever see its positive effects. Benefit finding can help. Researcher Kristen Riley describes benefit finding as "a reported positive life change resulting from the struggle to cope with a challenging life event such as trauma, illness, or other negative experiences."

Psychologist Tony Cassidy defines benefit finding as "the process of deriving positive growth from adversity." His research suggests that finding the positive amidst a negative experience can help people cope and manage stress. It represents a massive shift in positive psychology, highlighting that post-traumatic growth is possible—and that it all happens through positive reframing.

So, how do you do it?

Researchers Tomich & Helgeson, and McMillen & Fisher also developed frameworks to help us find benefits in periods of adversity. Tomich & Helgeson call their model the Benefit

Finding Scale. The scale identifies six benefits that one could find through trauma: acceptance, empathy, appreciation, family domain, positive self-view, and reprioritisation.

Many of these overlap with McMillen & Fisher's Perceived Benefit Scale, which identifies eight benefits: lifestyle changes, material gain, increases in self-efficacy, family closeness, community closeness, faith in people, compassion, and spirituality.

Here's an example of benefit finding in action. At one of our Virtual Gratitude Experiences™, an attendee named Mark shared his story. In 2020, right when the coronavirus pandemic hit the US, Mark's oldest daughter was diagnosed with cervical cancer.

Due to the pandemic, his company had gone fully remote, and he and his family were at home—including all of his grown children. Given all that was happening in the world, Mark's employer was very supportive, making it easy for him to take care of his daughter in his own home.

As such, the pandemic was actually a blessing for Mark and his family. If it hadn't happened, Mark said, it would have been impossible for all of them to be together during what would ultimately be his daughter's last few months of life.

If we were to look at both the Benefit Finding Scale and Perceived Benefit Scale, we would see that Mark learned acceptance, empathy, appreciation, family closeness, community closeness, compassion, and spirituality.

While the loss is undoubtedly a tragedy, the family experienced benefits that will continue to unfold over the course of their lives.

My friend Ron Carson always says "there's a gift in everything." It's the mantra he's used to help process past traumatic experiences, and find the benefits in them. Whereas others might have felt lucky to get out of some of the situations Ron found himself in, he was grateful that they happened in the first place.

By finding the benefits in his difficult experiences, and then giving gratitude to the ways he overcame them, he has been able to make them a part of his story and recognize the strengths that came out of them. Even better, he is using his story to inspire others.

Consider the benefits your most difficult moments have brought to bear, and what you can do to pay them forward.

## Gratitude Inquiry:

- *Reflection: According to the Benefit Finding Scale, there are six benefits one can find through trauma: acceptance, empathy, appreciation, family domain, positive self-view, and reprioritisation. Which of these have you experienced in your life?*

- *Reflection: Ron Carson taught us to be able to say "there's a gift in everything?" Where does this ring true, and where is it hard to accept in your life?*

- *Action: Complete the Benefits Finding Checklist below using an open memory from your past.What was that one negative experience in your life?Check off the boxes below of benefits that negative memory taught you.Tally up the score at the bottom of the exercise to determine how positive that memory actually is.Then complete the prompt at the bottom of the exercise.*

# Positive Benefits Checklist

☐ Empathy      ☐ Compassion

☐ Acceptance      ☐ Material gain

☐ Appreciation      ☐ Positive self-view

☐ Family closeness      ☐ Lifestyle changes

☐ Community closeness      ☐ Self-efficacy

☐ Faith in people      Score ☐ /11

I'm grateful that ______________ occurred, because it taught me ______________, ______________, ______________, and ______________.

# Pain into Connection

*"People heal from their pain when they have
an authentic connection with another human being."*
– Marshall B. Rosenberg

What do you do when something bad happens? If you tend to go inward or shut down, you're not alone.

Most people individualize the tough stuff in their lives. They focus on their own hurt. They hold it in. Further, they imagine that they're the only ones going through it. As such, they fail to recognize what has happened to people they know, love, and trust, and they aren't curious about what may have happened to their neighbor, either. That leads to stress and isolation.

But there's power in our pain, especially when it comes to connection. Tough times, trauma, and negativity can bring us together. Known to sociologists as "social glue," pain can behave like a binding agent in social settings, creating bonds between those who have experienced it. When people share gratitude for the painful moments they've been through—stories marked by regret, grief, adversity, or fear—they can become closer.

Many see adversity as a personal journey, something you have to get through on your own. On the contrary: adversity can help you become more open to others and find fulfillment through those connections.

When you stop hiding the tough situations you've been through and start processing them with others, you will find compassion, softness, love, and loyalty within your community. You will feel less alone, knowing that others have gone through similar struggles.

And when you reach out *while* you're struggling, you are poised to reap even more benefits—particularly if others are having a hard time too.

In his book *Tribe*, Sebastian Junger explained an intereting phenomenon: suicide and depression actually declined among people who found themselves in the middle of active conflict.

Before World War II broke out, experts predicted that as many as 4 million people in England would experience some kind of psychiatric breakdown as they grappled with the knowledge that Germany would be constantly attacking London. But as the forty-two-day Blitzkrieg progressed, psychiatric emergencies actually went down. Emergency services in London reported an average of only two cases of bomb neuroses a week. Depression rates for both men and women declined abruptly during the air raids on London as well.

Meanwhile, the rural outskirts of England—which experienced no violence at all—saw male depression rates rise rather than fall. Researcher Juan Pascual Leone hypothesized that these men were depressed because they couldn't participate in the struggle alongside their fellow countrymen.

Junger learned that collective struggle even has an impact on suicide rates. When European countries went to war, suicide rates dropped significantly. During World War II, American airborne units had some of the lowest psychiatric casualty rates of the entire US military. During the Irish Civil War, from 1969–1970, suicide rates in Belfast went down by 50 percent.

When people are actively engaged in a cause bigger than themselves, their lives have more purpose with a resulting improvement in mental health. But to feel those benefits, they must be on the front lines, demonstrating their commitment to the collective.

For this reason, though it may be hard to believe, people are going to miss the coronavirus pandemic. Adversity leads people to depend more on one another, and that closeness can produce a kind of nostalgia for hard times once they subside. To see this in action, one only needs to think back to the first few months of lockdown, when videos of people singing on Italian balconies with their neighbors or cheering for healthcare workers during a hospital shift change went viral.

What were they doing in those moments? Giving gratitude for the people in their communities who were keeping them sane and safe, respectively. We need to champion moments like those—moments that allow our communities to foster the resilience necessary to get through tough times.

When I went into the Javits Center in New York City in the early part of 2021, I witnessed one of the most remarkable moments of gratitude I've ever encountered. Thousands of people had shown up day after day to receive their COVID vaccine. Lines of people from all over the city snaked around the building. All of us were in the fight against the virus together, and it was humbling to be part of a system that was saving the lives of so many people. We showed up, got our shots, and did our part.

Upon receiving my vaccine, I burst into tears, thinking about the pain of the tens of thousands of our New York City neighbors who didn't live long enough to receive it—and the family members they left behind. I cried from the pain of almost losing my father to the very same virus.

But when those tears subsided, I felt grateful. I walked toward the exit of the Javits Center and saw a huge wall dedicated to words of gratitude. Volunteers had arranged pens and paper for people to write notes expressing their appreciation. The wall was blanketed in notes, all of which highlighted bright spots in what had been a sea of darkness. I turned the corner emotionally that day, and realized that there was great relief and pride to be found amidst our community. We were getting through the pandemic together.

By sharing your struggles, giving gratitude for the negative experiences you've had, and listening to others do the same, you can make it to the front lines of human connection and help ease the loneliness epidemic many of us are experiencing today.

The season one finale of Ted Lasso captures this phenomenon so well. The team has just been handed a rough loss that would force them to be demoted to a lesser football league, and they are huddled in the locker room mourning it. That's when Coach Lasso steps up.

He encourages his players not to face this adversity alone, but to feel the pain and to support each other through it.

"Please do me this favor, will you?" Lasso says. "Lift your heads up and look around this locker room. Look at everybody else in here. And I want you to be grateful you're going through this sad moment with all these other folks because, I promise you, there is something worse out there than being sad. And that is being alone and being sad. Ain't no one in this room alone." They would go on to find the benefits of that tough loss and become champions the next season.

We can all take a page from Lasso's playbook and make giving gratitude part of how we process pain.

So, take the L, share your pain, and be grateful for what you discover along the way. Chances are you'll be—and feel—better for it.

## Gratitude Inquiry:

- *Reflection: Who is someone you know who has seemed to encounter similar types of adversity as you? How has your connection blossomed through that struggle?*

- *Reflection: What aspects of the Covid 19 pandemic can you express gratitude for? Who did you meet through that struggle that you are now closer to?*

- *Action: Reach out to one person you share trauma bonds with and share with them the benefits of talking together about your shared experience.*

# Fear into Fortitude

*"Each of us must confront our own fears, must come
face to face with them. How we handle our fears
will determine where we go with the rest of our lives.
To experience adventure or to be limited by the fear of it."*
– Judy Blume

What do you do when your worst fears are realized? Going forward, do you avoid similar situations entirely, or do you lean in, ready to contend with what life may throw your way? Though doing so can be terrifying, diving in—and feeling grateful for the opportunity to do so—can be pretty powerful.

My team and I were in London producing a series of in-person Gratitude Dinners for a dear friend, Patrick Bosworth. We held a dinner for a different group of his colleagues each evening—all set on a houseboat on the River Thames. The first two dinners were phenomenal; they followed our recipe perfectly. But because of one guest's powerful story, the third was unforgettable.

Picture the setting for a moment: We're enjoying a meal on a houseboat in the shadow of the Tower Bridge, right around the bend from Borough Market, a famous foodie destination near Shakespeare's Globe. A spectacular setting is the icing on the cake, but, as you know by now, the key ingredient in our dinners is our Signature Gratitude Question: ***If you could give credit or thanks to one person in your life, someone you don't thank enough, who would that be?***

Usually, when the dinner party attendees hear that question, they take a collective breath as they consider it. It's quiet for a moment, and the space that silence provides serves as an invitation for them to leave the present, dive deep into the past, and pull forth amazing stories about the people who have helped them get to where they are today. What matters most is not the people they choose to be grateful for, but the vulnerability of expression—their willingness to publicly contend with an emotional experience.

During the third dinner in our houseboat series, a businessman shared his answer to our Signature Gratitude Question. He told us the story of an unfortunate scuba trip in the frigid North Atlantic, during which he nearly lost his life.

The dive began like any other, but when he surfaced from the depths of the ocean, the boat he had jumped from was gone. He was surrounded by nothing but open water. Hours passed without a sign of the boat. *What goes through one's brain in those terrifying moments? What scenes would you replay from your life?*

But the most compelling part of the story was not finding himself abandoned or the perilous period he spent alone in the water; it was what happened when he was saved.

A boat appeared on the horizon and the rescuers pulled him aboard. But before he could change out of his scuba gear and into dry clothes, the captain told the man to get back into the water—the same cold water that almost killed him. Warily, the man submerged himself in the frigid waters, and after five minutes of scuba diving, he got back on the boat.

Why did the captain do this to this man? Ordering a desperate diver who had just been near death back into the depths sounds sadistic. But I promise you, the captain was doing him a favor—and the man told us as much when he recounted the story.

There was a method to the captain's madness. His rationale was that by forcing the man to grapple with the deeply distressing situation he had just experienced, he wouldn't fear scuba diving for the rest of his life. Encouraging him to jump back into the water jump-started his healing, just like providing food, water and warmth brought him safety. The man was grateful to the captain not just for saving his life, but also for helping him combat fear.

Of course, certain traumas can take a lifetime to process. But when a fear-inducing or traumatic moment occurs in life, grateful processing can be a first step forward. Acknowledging the fear you felt can help you overcome it.

What does fear have to do with gratitude? Fear is a feeling that comes from a traumatic situation—one from your past, or perhaps one that you imagine could happen. If you feel fear, it's because your brain is telling you that there's something related that you haven't resolved.

We can't avoid negative experiences; and they will undoubtedly trigger fear from time to time. But we get to choose how we respond to them.

By recalling his experience—and expressing his gratitude for the captain's actions—the man could identify the positive outcomes that occurred as a result of that negative life experience.

Now, the experience transcends being a harrowing situation he merely survived; it's one that reaffirms his self-confidence, hope, pride, and optimism. He was rescued from the scariest situation he had ever encountered, and rather than avoid the water for the rest of his life, he immediately dove back in— thanks in large part to the captain who saved him. Further, the man's willingness to share his story that night was an act of gratitude in and of itself.

The ripples continued: he gave the other guests the benefit of observing him and shared his gratitude (we'll talk about the power of observation later). And though I cannot say so with certainty, I wouldn't be surprised to learn that numerous attendees benefited from new friendships—the man included— as a result of his willingness to tell his story.

Finally, each time he tells the story, he confronts his fears— and those who recount what they heard from him do the same.

You can use a similar strategy to face your fear, and then apply gratitude to overcome it.

## Gratitude Inquiry:

- *Reflection: Have you experienced a situation where your worst fears were realized? How has your approach to that type of situation shifted since that encounter?*

- *Reflection: What are some fears you have been hesitant to acknowledge or name? Where does that fear come from? What's the worst that could happen? And is it really as bad as I'm imagining?*


- *Action: Write about or share with others your story of overcoming fear, just like the story of the scuba diver.*

# Anger into Compassion

*"In compassion, when we feel with the other, we dethrone ourselves from the center of our world and we put another person there."*
– Karen Armstrong

In early 2021, my girlfriend Molly and I were robbed by someone who lived on the corner of our street. I was actually home at the time, which made for quite a traumatic moment. We confronted each other, and he immediately took off running with my stolen goods. I let the police intervene, he was eventually captured, and justice prevailed.

A few months later, Molly and I were walking along the pier when we watched someone step onto its edge and prepare to jump. As we looked closer, I realized it was the partner-in-crime of the man who robbed us. I'd seen them together on our block many times.

That realization, let alone the events unfolding in front of me, could have kept me frozen in place. There must have been 300 people watching from the park lawn, but no one was moving.

I couldn't stand by and watch. I sprinted over and made eye contact, letting him know I was there. We didn't exchange any words, but I was able to distract him.

One might assume the robbery had made enough of a negative impact on me that I wouldn't feel compelled to help this person. But besides not wanting to let resentment harden my heart, I also had chosen to process the robbery with gratitude months prior.

On the day of the robbery, I was forced to reschedule two business calls. Those delayed calls eventually resulted in closed deals—and massive wins for my company. The clients I spoke with that day heard a vulnerable part of my story, and met me with empathy. That helped us connect on a much deeper level. They understood what my team and I were doing, and that inspired them to work with us.

Of course, I did not choose to be robbed in my own home. But I knew it was ultimately my responsibility to manage my emotions after the fact. I chose to process them with gratitude, and ended up making peace with the situation. The robbery also brought me closer to my neighbors, as every one of them offered tips to the police about the situation. And because I processed the situation with gratitude, it was easy to approach this person with compassion and courage. After all, his friend has brought more into my life than he'd taken away.

*If given the choice, would you choose compassion over resentment?* It could save your life, or someone else's. And if you're not yet there, gratitude can help.

# Gratitude Inquiry:

- *Reflection: When is it hard for you to show compassion to others? What kind of situations trigger resentment?*

- *Reflection: When have you seen compassion change someone else's life?*

- *Action: Write down the name of one person in your life who you need to show compassion to, and what is the compassionate sentence that you want to say to them?*

# Regret into Progress

*"Make the most of your regrets; never smother your sorrow, but tend and cherish it till it comes to have a separate and integral interest. To regret deeply is to live afresh."*
– Henry David Thoreau

It might seem strange to offer gratitude to our deepest regrets. Regrets are often sources of pain and frustration. We find ourselves dwelling on the unfortunate circumstances of our lives—a bad investment, poor career choice, or the one who got away.

But what we don't realize is that regret helps us to remember what, and who, we truly care about. By acknowledging our regrets—especially in community with others—we get in touch with our values, giving us a chance to make new decisions that align with what we genuinely want. This allows us to give gratitude to the choices we *did* make, and the positive outcomes that occurred as a result. That's the place where we can begin to process and find gratitude.

In August of 2021, my friend Ron Carson called and asked if I could come to Omaha, Nebraska, to help him and his team produce a day-long offsite on the topic of gratitude. The day was to be magical, with hundreds of company stakeholders flying in to participate.

The morning began with acai bowls and twelve senior leaders huddled together to chat gratitude. With the help of the magical Kelsey Ruwe, Chief of Staff at Carson Group, we came up with a special prompt for this group: *What's one experience you regret giving up on too soon in life?*

I knew that Ron's team was courageous enough to go there, and that the conversations that arose from this question would be powerful.

One team member shared about never venturing out of their state. Now that they had kids and a busy home life, they felt as if it were too late to do much traveling. One of them regretted not going to medical school. He had come from a long line of doctors, and by choosing to pursue business, he felt as if he'd flunked out and let them down. Another regretted giving up on a relationship after the other person said some hurtful things. One of them even shared about the regret they felt for not speaking up publicly about being abused as a young child.

The participants were vulnerable and brave. Many of them offered up truths they hadn't even shared with their families. After everyone spoke, the group wondered where they would have been now if they had acted differently.

But instead of harping on what they could have done differently, and what would have happened as a result, I placed a stack of paper and some pens on the table and asked them to write down all the benefits that had come from what they *did* do. Then, I set a timer for five minutes and watched the magic unfold.

On the other side of the exercise, they realized that, while they were curious about what their lives would have looked like if they had made different decisions, the gift was that they couldn't actually know.

To dwell in the "what-ifs" would have meant missing out on all they had experienced as a result of the path they traveled. And looking over the lists they had just made, they could appreciate all they had in that moment, as individuals and as a team. They were sitting in a room of safe peers and colleagues. They had made significant strides on their own and together. They had built authentic personal and professional relationships. They had gotten to know themselves through their high and low points and what they had learned from each one. The experiences they carried with them had made them better parents, better friends, and better colleagues. And when they looked at all they had done with the choices they made, they forgave themselves properly for those regrets.

I've had to grapple with my own set of regrets, of course. People often ask me how I do it, overcoming the things that could otherwise hold me back. My answer?

I own the things that once gave me shame. And I give gratitude to them.

When they ask me about my decisions and regrets, people often point to the fact that I didn't graduate from college. Of course, I'll never know what my life would have been like if I'd gotten that degree—the people I'd have met, the jobs I could've held, and so on. But I flip that experience on its head. Instead of being consumed with what *didn't* happen as a result of not finishing college, I focus on what *did* happen.

I made it part of my story, a story that nobody can ever take away from me. Of course, there were painful points—pain is inevitable. But pain is inherently human and beautiful. There's value in it, and if you look, you'll find it.

The process of grappling with your regret, and overcoming any guilt and shame associated with it, will likely make you very emotional. It isn't going to be easy. But there's value in those emotions too—they're a form of power, of courage, of bravery. When you tap into those emotions, you're tapping into progress.

And when you're grateful for them, you realize all that you've received, rather than what you've lost.

That doesn't mean the regrets won't come—we all have them. Any choice we make requires giving up the alternative routes we might have taken. But those who are grateful are better able to reconcile the perceived losses that come from making one decision or another and move forward.

## Gratitude Inquiry:

- *Reflection: When do you find yourself dwelling on the "what-if's" in life?*


- *Reflection: What's one experience you regret giving up on too soon in life?*


- *Action: Make a list of all the benefits that came from the above situation and the life path you chose. Have any of these contributed positively to the person you are today?*

# Grief into Legacy

*"Happiness is beneficial for the body, but it is grief
that develops the powers of the mind."*
– Marcel Proust

My friend Susan Ganeshan told me a powerful story about how she used gratitude to overcome grief in her life.

Susan grew up as the youngest and only girl in a family of four children. Tragically, her older brother Dean died by suicide at age twenty-one. The suicide was devastating for the entire family, but especially for their mother.

Susan's mother internalized Dean's suicide as a personal failure. She wondered how she had let such a thing happen. Ruminating on the loss and her role in it made her distant. But eventually, she realized what had happened wasn't about her at all; it had everything to do with Dean and how he experienced the world.

When Susan's mother realized that, she underwent a transformation, becoming a loving, giving, and grateful person who appreciated every moment she had left. She decided to honor her son by being more present in her life and in the lives of others—giving more love, more praise, and more hugs to her children and others in her community. Susan said her mother's transformation wasn't limited to a few years after Dean's death. Her mother never stopped showing up for herself and others. She spent the rest of her life making sure to appreciate all that she had and to let others know what they meant to her.

Susan shared with me that she was grateful for that lesson so early in life. She was grateful that she had the opportunity to see the difference that giving hugs, gratitude, and love can make in one's own life and in the lives of others—particularly when that generosity of spirit comes from grief. That lesson was a bright light that emerged from tragedy.

"What part of Dean's legacy lives on in you?" I asked her.

She told me that she had been proud of Dean's service record. He was in the Army, where he was training to become a medic. And he was always there for her. She remembered fondly the times that he would drive twenty miles across town just to spend half an hour teaching her how to drive stick.

To honor his life, she has dedicated hers to helping people, and being there for them in their time of need. Today, she looks to appreciate the small things in life and pay them forward, eagerly giving people the gift of her presence.

The gratitude she felt for Dean also turned into a formal gratitude practice of her own. Every day, she wakes up and writes down three to ten things for which she's grateful.

In 2021, her mother died of COVID. And thanks to her gratitude practice, Susan found that she could still find beauty in the world around her and see grace in the way things had played out.

Her mother had recently been diagnosed with a terminal illness, with which she likely would have struggled for years. COVID saved her mother years of agony, and brought Susan and her siblings together for fifteen days—the longest they'd spent in one another's company in their entire adult lives.

Through their commitment to gratitude, both Susan and her mother tapped into its ability to heal. Leading trauma clinician and researcher Bessel Van der Kolk speaks to gratitude's ability to heal trauma and overcome grief. He explains that "states and thoughts of appreciation take our system into coherence. Hence gratitude is healing." I know how difficult it sounds, but grieving with gratitude can make the darkest times in life a little more manageable.

Author Kelly Buckley outlined a few ways to manage grief with gratitude, which she developed after losing her twenty-three-year-old son.

1. Cry your heart out. Crying doesn't make us weak. Instead, it's an act of acceptance—one that makes us aware of our emotions. It helps us let go of some of the pain and take steps to change our lives.
2. Collect the broken pieces. Grieving with gratitude lets us appreciate the things we still have. For example, someone who just lost their job may want to take time to give gratitude to the community who is supporting him through the loss. Recognizing all they provide can supply the motivation necessary to move on and begin searching for a new opportunity.
3. Ask for help. Sometimes, we can't do it all on our own. A professional can help you understand why you're struggling so much and identify how best to cope. Studies have shown that people who practice gratitude are more willing to

participate in counseling and therapy for managing their depression, and the prognosis is much brighter in such instances.

4. Keep a gratitude jar. Keep a clear jar or box in a spot you frequent, along with some slips of paper and a pen. Every day, grab a new slip and write about what you're grateful for that day—a loved one, your health, an opportunity, or even your own strength. You'll find that as you fill the jar you'll feel more fulfilled.

The grief will still be there, but you will gain the strength to look beyond it.

Our friend Sandy Gibson lost his father at ten years old, his mother at eleven years old, and was adopted by his older half-brother when he was just twelve years old. Looking back, he said, "I'm grateful. I looked at my parents dying and kinda realized, if you can get through that as an eleven year old, you can probably get through a fair amount of hardship and failure as an adult."

He has gone on to raise $55 million for his newest startup, through which he's upending the $20 billion funeral parlor and cemetery business.

Today, he does things to remember his parents and how grateful he is for the time he had with them. He watches baseball on the regular because it reminds him of his father (more on that later). He serves on the board of the nonprofit his mother created when she was alive. And now he's working to help the next generation celebrate their loved ones' lives in meaningful ways. *Would any of that impact have been possible if he hadn't experienced such great tragedy early on?*

# Gratitude Inquiry:

- *Reflection: Who has left an imprint on your life through their legacy?*


- *Reflection: What is a dark moment of grief in your life that seems impossible to approach with gratitude?*


- *Action: Choose one of Kelly Buckley's ways to manage grief with gratitude and try one out this week.*

# The South Star Principle

*"God allows us to experience the low points in life in order to teach us lessons that we could learn in no other way."*
–C.S. Lewis

It was March of 2021, and I had just left my father's hospital bed for the umpteenth time that week. I was home to connect virtually with a woman named Cate. As much as I didn't want to be there, I was obsessed with Cate's company, and our mutual friend, Kerry, said we would hit it off famously.

When I joined the call, Cate was waiting, but her camera was off. She promptly spoke up. "Sorry, I've been on ten back-to-back meetings today. I just need a break from the camera."

I'd read studies about the detrimental impact of spending whole days on Zoom, so I went along with it. At that point, I was just grateful she showed up. But when she began to tell me her story, I could hear her pain.

She launched her self-funded startup—a membership-based career and personal growth platform and collaboration hub for women, (and their male allies) across all professional journeys, in the middle of Manhattan—just before COVID began. She took over a huge lease for a beautiful office building. And then the world shut down.

I could feel the pressure Cate was under on our call. Million-dollar office lease, thousands of members starving for connection, and the stress of having to appear on screen for fourteen hours per day.

So, I looked at my dark screen and said, "Cate, do you mind if I ask a question?"

"Sure," she said hesitantly. I posed our Signature Gratitude Question: ***If you could give credit or thanks to one person in your life, that you don't give enough credit or thanks to, who would that be?***

She proceeded to tell me that she'd like to thank an ex-boss from her previous career in banking. This person was a horrible manager, always put her down, and frequently doubted her abilities as a leader. But this ex-boss had made her realize she needed to quit banking to do her own thing—to help other professional women gain access to good leaders, to people who believed in them.

"Do you think about him often?" I asked.

"I do. I like to remind myself of all of his bad qualities, so I can do the opposite." Essentially, she had a list of who she *didn't* want to be in life. I could hear the relief in her voice as she identified the benefits of that relationship. She had made the decision to move forward for herself, and to change the game for other women, so they wouldn't have to struggle with the same issues she'd faced.

It was validating to help her find that relief, and as I leaned back in my chair, I said, "It sounds like you have a good South Star." I had made it up on the spot, but the concept stuck with us.

See, so often in life, we focus on a North Star—what we're aiming to fulfill or achieve. Michael Ofei defines one's North

Star as, "your personal mission statement. It's a fixed destination that you can depend on in your life as the world changes around you." A North Star is something that you strive for—that mission helps you make daily decisions that keep you on track.

And while North Stars are great, they're also quite the luxury. Not everyone knows where they want to go. When life looks gloomy and feels turbulent, and you can't see how you'll get out of your current circumstances, how can you identify a North Star—or take the steps to follow it?

Sometimes you must do the opposite. Sometimes you need to figure out where you *don't* want to go in life, and let that knowledge drive you forward as you figure out ways to avoid doing just that.

This is where the South Star principle comes in. Cate was so grateful for that terrible boss because he had inspired her to pinpoint exactly who she *didn't* want to be as a manager. Once she considered those negative behaviors, it was easy to avoid them, because the stakes were so high. Every time she would find herself doing something on that list, she worked to find strategies to do the opposite.

She could also recognize how far she'd come. Her current life was a far cry from that of the woman stuck working for that bad boss. And her South Star kept her moving forward. As she shared with Dot.LA, "You have got to make your mark and, you know what, you are going to get pushed down a million times in your life. The defining part is can you get back up and just keep going."

It's evidence that giving gratitude to the people who have held you back—and identifying what you don't want—can keep you moving forward.

# Gratitude Inquiry:

- *Reflection: Do you have a North Star in life, a fixed destination of something you're striving for?*

- *Reflection: What are a few qualities you despise in some people around you?*

- *Action: Write down a list of 5 moments when you've accidentally lived the qualities you despise in others.*

# Become the Man in the Hole

*"I want to stand as close to the edge
as I can without going over. Out on the edge you see
all kinds of things you can't from the center."*
– Kurt Vonnegut

Author Kurt Vonnegut developed a theory about stories as part of his rejected master's thesis in anthropology.

He posited that stories have shapes, which can be drawn as graphs. Studying these recurring story shapes, Vonnegut said, can teach us as much about a society as studying its physical artifacts.

Vonnegut found that some of the most popular narratives in the history of humanity involve a dip from good fortune to ill fortune, with a final redemptive arc that brings a protagonist to new heights. He called that shape "the man in the hole."

Now, these stories don't need to be about men, and they don't have to involve holes, but the premise is as follows: the protagonist gets into trouble, then gets out again, and ends up better for the experience. The struggle enables others to see themselves in the protagonist.

I myself became the man in the hole recently. I told my online community a story I share in this book as well: that I can't remember fifteen years of my life. It was vulnerable as heck to share that so publicly; after all, I had a lot of pain and shame associated with being so heavily medicated as a child.

But you know what happened? DMs and texts started rolling in, one kinder and more supportive than the next. *Dude,* one message read, *I can't remember my childhood either, and I didn't know what it was until I read your post.*

With each note, I climbed farther out of my hole—and I know many of my friends and colleagues got a boost as well.

Therein lies the power of telling our stories. I'm not saying it's easy. It takes vulnerability and a willingness to look at every aspect of our lives—even the challenging moments—with gratitude for what we've learned and how we've been shaped. Through those efforts, though, we get to feel connected to others. We build relationships and empathy. We inspire others to share their stories too. That makes it all worth it. When you're in the hole—when you're at your low point—gratitude is the tool that can get you out.

Remember the classic Christmas movie, *It's a Wonderful Life?* George Bailey is on the brink of ending his life due to financial ruin. His business partner lost $8,000, and creditors are about to throw him in jail for fraud. He walks to a local bridge and prepares to jump to his death, when an angel intervenes.

George wishes that he was never born, and the angel shows him all that would have happened if that had been the case. George witnesses his wife struggling for money, his best friend becoming an alcoholic, and the members of his community descend into chaos. When he understands all that has happened as a product of his existence, he is left with a deep appreciation and gratitude for everyone and everything he has—even the struggles.

The angel brings him back to the present moment, and George runs through his town screaming about how grateful he is to be there.

Sometimes, it takes years to give gratitude for the time you've spent in the hole. Just look at Steve Jobs. He knew what he wanted to do early in life, starting Apple in his parents' garage with his partner, Steve Wozniak, when he was just twenty-one. They worked hard, and over a decade, they grew Apple from two employees to over 4,000. At thirty, Steve Jobs was king of the world. He had just released their prized creation, Lisa, the first computer with a graphical interface, when he was fired from his own company. Ouch.

He became the man in the hole. What had been his focus for most of his life was gone, and it was devastating. For a while, he didn't know what to do. He thought about running away from Silicon Valley and slinking off into nothingness.

But it began to dawn on him: He had been rejected by his own company, but he was still in love with the work—and with the impact he had made to date.

So he decided to start over. He didn't know it at the time, but getting fired from Apple would be the best thing that had ever happened to him. The heaviness that had come with success was replaced by the lightness of beginning again—with the humility, eagerness to learn, and the hopeful uncertainty that came with it.

He would enter the most creative period of his life in the years that followed, founding a few companies, and even falling in love with the woman who would become his wife. One of his companies, Pixar, would go on to create the world's first computer-animated feature film, Toy Story, and become the most successful animation studio in the world.

When Apple bought one of his companies, NeXT, he would return to the helm of his first operation and build it into the trillion-dollar monster it is now.

Jobs was very vocal about how grateful he was for being fired from Apple. He called it his "awful-tasting medicine," but it was just what the doctor ordered.

Sometimes life hits you in the head with a brick and you find yourself at the bottom of that hole. Don't lose faith in your long-term vision. Stay committed to doing what you love, or to finding your path. If you believe you can get out of the hole, you're going to get out of it. And when you do, you're going to have an amazing story to share.

Remember, too, that it's not when you're riding high and life is going swimmingly that you create meaningful moments of connection. It's when you're down in the dumps and people can see the human in you. And when you're grateful for those moments, they become even more powerful.

## Gratitude Inquiry:

- *Reflection: What's an example of a time when friends or community helped you climb out of a hole?*

- *Reflection: Have you seen a friend experience what Steve Jobs called "awful-tasting medicine," a painful situation that put them in the hole? What was the long-term outcome of that situation?*

- *Action: Paint a picture describing your life before a tragic moment, then paint a picture describing your life down in that tragic hole. Finally, paint a picture of the new heights you've reached by getting out of that hole.*

# Connect the Dots Backwards

*"You can't connect the dots looking forward; you can only connect them looking backwards. So you have to trust that the dots will somehow connect in your future. You have to trust in something—your gut, destiny, life, karma, whatever."*
– Steve Jobs

I've already told you a bit about Steve Jobs, but I didn't tell you about what we have in common. Like Steve, I decided to drop out of college. And, like Steve, unsure of what to do next, I decided to spend the next eighteen months of my life floating.

So, why did he drop out—and why did I? For Steve, it started before he was even born. His biological mother was a young, unwed graduate student and decided to put him up for adoption.

She was convinced that she would be a terrible mother, and wanted to give her son a better chance at success. She searched around and eventually found a set of parents to adopt Steve—wealthy people with advanced degrees, whom she thought could give him a better life. But when they had the chance to adopt a girl, they backed out.

The husband and wife who were next in line were working-class people. They didn't have much money, but they made one promise: to send him to college.

At the age of seventeen, he would indeed go to college. His parents were prepared to spend all of their savings on his tuition. But when he got there, it just didn't feel right.

The same was true for me. College plunged me into a general sense of malaise, and led me to alcohol, drugs, car crashes, and even brief stints in jail. I was a shell of a human being, not only because my actions were destroying my body and my relationships, but because I—like Steve—had no idea what I wanted to do with my life and no idea how college was going to help me figure it out.

How were we going to tell our parents that we didn't appreciate the opportunity that they had worked so hard to give us?

Steve decided to drop out and trust that it would all work out. Meanwhile, I was served papers by my father and given a choice of which rehab to attend to fix my problems.

The decision transformed our lives.

The minute Steve dropped out, he stopped taking the required classes that didn't hold his attention and began attending the ones that looked far more compelling. He didn't have a dorm room or a meal plan, so he bunked with friends and bought food with the money he got from turning in Coke® bottles. And every Sunday night, he would walk the seven miles across town to get one good meal at the Hari Krishna temple. Much of what he stumbled across during that time by following his curiosity and intuition turned out to be priceless later on.

When I left college, I cleared away the things that didn't serve me, like fraternity life, college politics, and my international business major. And in their stead—after a long stint in rehab—I began focusing on my love of the great outdoors. While Steve stuck around his campus and audited classes, I returned to a place I'd known since birth: Hilton Head Island. This time, though, I came back as a kayak tour guide and boat captain working for Outside Hilton Head, leading tourists through nature. I learned how much I loved leading groups, learning from people, and helping them tell their stories. Those elements—the stuff I was truly interested in life—became the foundation of my career years later.

But before I knew how things would turn out, I moved up to New York City on a whim at the behest of a grandmother figure in my life. I didn't have a college degree, or a job, or even a suitcase. I took up residence on a buddy's couch in Brooklyn, unsure of what I'd do, or how I'd make any money, but because I trusted the non-linear nature of my life—and the skills I'd developed in the process—I knew that my move to New York City would somehow work out.

Steve said that "you can't connect the dots looking forward, you can only connect them looking backwards." You've just got to trust that the dots will connect down the line. Whether by gut, amor fati, prayer, or karma, you have to believe that things will work out—just as they did for Steve, and for me.

Giving gratitude to the non-linear ways that my life has unfolded brings me tremendous joy today, and when I look back, it all makes sense.

When we connect the dots backwards, and give gratitude to super-specific points on our path, we realize that all of us have had to overcome our own set of challenges. When we give gratitude to these experiences in the company of others—sharing our stories, trials, and tribulations and how beautifully it all worked out in the end—we build meaningful connections.

Just the other week, I was sitting in a car on the way to the airport. I had just spent the morning reading a 112-page research paper by Sara Algoe on the witnessing effect. The more I read that paper, the more I realized that we were already instinctively and intuitively building models in our business around the very concepts she explored.

I got giddy in that cab. Then, my giddiness turned to tears. I was overwhelmed with immense gratitude for the non-linear life I led, and how it all made sense in retrospect.

The dots connected backwards. That non-linear life helped develop the skills and sense to build models to serve people at their most vulnerable, in ways that scientists would prove to be effective.

And when you give gratitude for the struggles that only make sense in the rearview mirror, you'll find hope and pride in all that you've accomplished and all that you can achieve—and inspire it in others.

## Gratitude Inquiry:

- *Reflection: Who's story of nonlinearity do you relate to in your own story, like I related my story to Steve Jobs?*

- *Reflection: In what ways has your life been linear? How has your life been non-linear? What positive benefits would you attribute to the non-linearity of your life?*

- *Action: Give gratitude to one dot in your life that unexpectedly worked out for the better.*

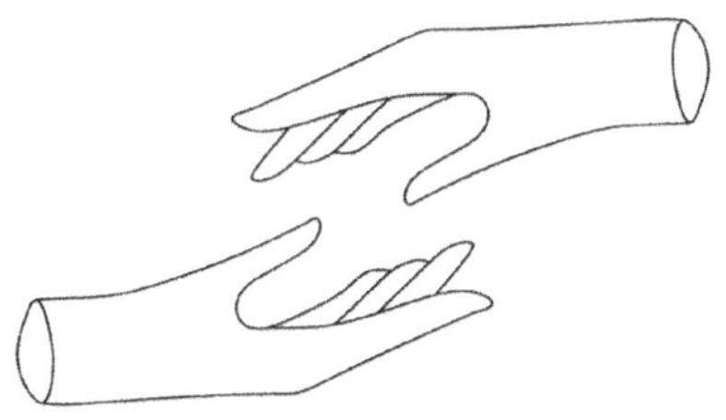



# To Give and to Receive

*“Silent gratitude isn’t very much to anyone.”*
– Gertrude Stein

# Gratitude Is Prosocial

*"The deepest craving of human nature
is the need to be appreciated."*
– William James

Gratitude is social by nature. It's us realizing that many—if not all—of the goodness in our lives comes from other people. Those moments that you thought of in the previous section, they were all filled with people who gave you a tremendous amount of value, or benefits.

Many people confuse gratitude with being "glad," or a sense of "luck" or "fate."

Sometimes people think they feel grateful due to a particular condition—good weather on a picnic day, for instance—but what they're feeling isn't gratitude. While the sunshine is certainly a gift, Barbara Fredrickson argues that the attendees aren't grateful, but rather glad it didn't rain, or perhaps lucky that they chose the day they did.

Instead, as Fredrickson explains, "to be grateful is to be grateful to someone."

Gratitude is a deeply social emotion. It's how we relate to each other, and thus, gratitude must be given to another individual. People feel grateful when they receive some sort of a benefit, big or small, from an actual person. When we express gratitude, we reflect kindness back to the person who ignited those feelings of gratitude in us. This forms a dyadic relationship: a relationship between two people.

If you find yourself at a picnic on a beautiful day, be grateful to the person who invited you—to the person who chose such a perfect day to connect over lunch. That will help cultivate a powerful bond between you two. But the impact may extend much farther.

Adam Grant reports that "behaviorally, gratitude is a prosocial trait that motivates individuals to engage in prosocial behaviors to reciprocate the assistance they receive from others." In other words, when gratitude is shared, people are inspired to pay it back—and pay it forward.

Plus, expressing gratitude feels good—and it's good for your health. The UC Davis Health study I mentioned previously found that "two pro-social gratitude activities per day (gratitude letter writing, etc.) reduced the risk of depression in at-risk patients by 41 percent over a six month period."

We become less depressed and more socially connected when we know that our actions are having a positive impact on others. The individual benefits of gratitude are amplified when you see its power to not just improve your own life, but also to strengthen a community bond and culture. By sharing your gratitude, you have the power to create meaningful experiences for others, creating a chain reaction of positive responses.

But to experience the full benefits of gratitude—and extend them to others—we must understand how to give it, receive it, and observe it.

# Gratitude Inquiry:

- *Reflection: Besides "glad," "luck," or "fate," what other words or feelings do you misassociate with gratitude?*

- *Reflection: Are there moments in your life when you've felt grateful for someone but didn't tell them? Why not? What got in the way?*

- *Action: Spend five days in a row completing two pro-social gratitude activities per day and write about how this impacts your health and wellbeing.*

# If You're Grateful,
# Give It Away

*"The worthiest way to give thanks for our blessings isn't to hog them, but to give them away."*
– Lynne Twist

Have you ever kept a gratitude journal, writing down the things you're grateful for, or even making a mental list each morning? While giving thanks in a journal, or in a self-reflective practice is good, giving it to others is better.

Why?

At its core, giving gratitude is an act of kindness. Grateful people are truly interested in helping others by letting them know they value what someone else has given them.

Unfortunately, it can be tricky to give gratitude authentically in this day and age. Many people fear that if they are too "good" of a person—too giving, or too grateful—they will become a doormat. I've seen friends worry that they are being too empathetic or too trusting. As a result, when a business deal goes sour they immediately think they've been taken advantage of for being too nice, rather than locating the true cause of the deal's dissolution.

The good news is that—contrary to the adage—nice people often finish *first*. I told you about Adam Grant's groundbreaking book, *Give and Take*, and the revelation that givers are "other-ish," valuing the good in people around them and focused on doing good by others without subverting their own needs. One way they do that is by giving gratitude.

If you're hesitant to share how you feel, consider this your sign to stop holding back. We assume that the people in our lives know how we feel about them. Researcher Dr. David Ludden explains that we often think, "Surely they know how grateful I am; I wouldn't want to embarrass them by getting so emotional."

Psychologists call this "egocentric bias." It's the notion that since something (in this case, our gratitude) is obvious to us, we assume it must be obvious to those around us. We end up believing that, when we thank our spouses for a home-cooked meal on a Tuesday night, for instance, they must know how much we appreciate *everything* they do. We figure they must understand that we're also thanking them for putting their career on pause to move across the country and be a stay-at-home dad, and for the kindness they show our kids on a daily basis, and for the love and care they have for us too. It's obvious, right?

But nothing is ever obvious. Assuming things only serves to create disconnection. When you don't tell people you're grateful for the things they do—big and small—they assume you're ungrateful, and they will start to slowly show you less benefits over time.

Researchers Amit Kumar and Nicholas Epley actually demonstrated that individuals undervalue the positive impact of their expressions of gratitude in a 2018 experiment. Kumar and Epley asked participants to write and send letters of gratitude and to predict the recipients' reaction: how surprised they would be to receive the letters, how positive their mood would be after they read them, how awkward they would feel to be shown such gratitude, etc. The researchers then surveyed the letter recipients on their reactions.

It turned out that the writers underestimated how much the letters would improve recipients' moods and overestimated how awkward they'd feel. The recipients were genuinely surprised to receive the letter—more so than predicted—and rather than feeling awkward, they felt very good to have received the giver's gratitude.

But these misconceptions about whether their gratitude would have an impact seem to deter people from showing it in the first place. Amit and Nicholas write that "underestimating the value of prosocial actions, such as expressing gratitude, may keep people from engaging in behavior that would maximize their own—and others'—well-being."

Isn't it a shame that we often take for granted how much expressing our gratitude would mean to others—to the detriment of our collective well-being?

That's why, at our Virtual Gratitude Experiences™, when people would answer our Signature Gratitude Question and talk about someone close to them—like a mother, father, spouse, sibling, or close friend; we'd actually have them pick up the phone and call that person on the spot. We know how much that phone call could mean to both parties, and so we do our best to make sure it happens.

An attendee at one of the experiences we produced in partnership with a Fortune 50 company even said that our experience prompted her to text a couple of her college roommates about some specific things that she was thankful for, right then. She said one of them texted her back and said, "Your note brought a tear to the eye. It's going in my memory box."

Now, let's say that the person to whom you'd like to give gratitude passed on before you were able to thank them for all they did for you. Let's say it's a grandfather who drove you to soccer practice every day, and now you are a professional soccer player. But you never thanked that great man for giving you the chance to pursue your passion.

If you can't give that gratitude to him, what should you do with all that generative and authentic energy? You should pay it forward, in his honor. After all, gratitude is as much about paying it forward as it is about giving back.

You can keep your grandfather's legacy alive by telling others about the ways in which he was there for you, and investing in them the way he invested in you. Do it for more than one person, and you'll amplify the benefits you received exponentially.

How?

Paying it forward is very contagious. Has a stranger ever paid for your coffee in a drive-through line? You couldn't thank them, so what did you do? You paid for the next person. You doing this for others is an act of gratitude, and it has power.

# Gratitude Inquiry:

- *Reflection: What is a time in life when you've been afraid to be too "good" of a person – too giving or too grateful – because you are afraid of becoming a doormat?*

- *Reflection: When have you seen "nice people" finish first in life?*

- *Action: Write about a time where you've seen gratitude become contagious in a social network, further amplifying the benefits you originally received.*

# Send a Gift,
# Shred the Receipt

*"The book-keeping of benefits is simple: it is all expenditure;
if any one returns it, that is clear gain; if he does not
return it, it is not lost, I gave it for the sake of giving."*
– Seneca

In 2021, Tony Safoian, the president and CEO of SADA Systems Inc., embarked on a powerful gratitude journey. He made donations on behalf of every one of the company's clients—more than 3,000 of them—supporting the causes they cared about to demonstrate how much he appreciated them.

After a call with Tony, I was inspired to do the same. I called up 186 of my clients, and asked them to share the names of local nonprofits that meant something to them. When they responded, I made a donation to the organization they shared. It was one way that I expressed my gratitude for our relationship.

But here's the thing: I kept no records of those donations. I didn't tell my clients that I'd made a donation. I burned the receipts. I didn't even deduct the amount I'd given from my taxes. Instead, I gave for the sake of giving.

What was the point, other than giving for giving's sake?

The next time I want to be generous or show my appreciation for my clients, I won't just be able to check out a spreadsheet, rinse, and repeat. I'll need to pick up the phone and call.

I've made burning receipts a regular practice in my life. I do it when I send a gift or write a letter to someone I care about. I don't want my giving—or my gratitude—to be complicated by expectations. I don't want to get caught up in an endless cycle of thank-you notes for thank-you notes. I don't need to get what I give back. That would be reciprocity, not generosity. And while reciprocity has its own value in life; it's sufficient, efficient, and meaningful just to give.

## Gratitude Inquiry:

- *Reflection: When was the last time you gave simply for the sake of giving, with no recognition from others? How did that make you feel?*

- *Reflection: Where in your life do you find yourself keeping records of benefits given, rather than just leaning into a giving nature?*

- *Action: Give an anonymous gift this week and don't tell anyone about it.*

# Give Gratitude to Weak Ties

*"By cultivating rich social networks, by cultivating weak ties, not just close ties but the weak ties, by becoming connectors and by connecting others so that they connect us, we create a world in which these self-amplifying feedback loops feed on top of each other."*
– Jason Silva

Are you grateful to someone you're not that close to, or don't see very often?

During our Gratitude Experiences, we often hear people express gratitude for those with whom they don't interact frequently—or even at all. They share the impact made on their lives by people they had known long ago, or those whom they didn't know very well. The problem is, because they aren't close to those people, they haven't reached out to let them know how much they mean to them.

We make all kinds of excuses to avoid the perceived awkwardness of giving gratitude, especially to people from our past. *What if they don't remember us? What if we didn't mean as much to them as they meant to us? What if, what if, what if.* We fear reaching out because we doubt that they found value in connecting with us in the first place. That lack of initiative—and gratitude—leads to loneliness, isolation, regret, and shame.

And that lack of gratitude, or ingratitude, if you will, was weighing heavy on my shoulders on December 30, 2021. I felt that I had become so bad at giving gratitude, despite being surrounded by it on a daily basis. I had all the tools to appreciate myself and others, but I rarely showed it. I convinced myself I was a fraud. *Who was I to extoll the benefits of gratitude when I failed to practice it in a meaningful way myself?*

That thought process led me down a scary and dangerous path, one that so many others had traveled.

But it didn't have to be that way. There are plenty of people just a phone call away who would have loved hearing from me—just like they'll enjoy hearing from you.

Gratitude bridges the gaps that have grown between people. The high school math teacher who inspired you to become an engineer. The coach whose early belief in you continues to influence your approach to tough projects even today. Your childhood best friend's mom who created a safe space for you to hang out after school—away from the chaos of your own home. Trust me, they all want to hear from you.

Don't underestimate the value of seemingly loose connections, either—what sociologists refer to as "weak ties." In a Stanford University paper entitled, "The Strength of Weak Ties," researchers found that social networks composed of weak ties were actually most effective when it came to sharing information. In other words, the people to whom you haven't spoken in years, are actually the most prone to pass on vital information for you.

Others' findings reinforce this assertion. In 1973, the sociologist Mark Granovetter found that 82 percent of professionals found new jobs through a contact that they saw only occasionally or rarely. In her book, "The Lost Art of Connecting," Susan MacPherson explained that people who have a broad network of weaker ties were more likely to be successful than those with fewer, closer connections.

Further, these ties can help us improve our perspectives. In Brian Uzzi and Shannon Dunlap's article, "How to Build a Network," they write that, "Highly diverse network ties can help you develop more complete, creative, and unbiased views of issues." I'm sure you can see the many ways in which that can be a major asset in work and beyond.

Reinvesting in these relationships could also have a snowball effect: They could open the door to other connections with whom you had lost touch and to entire branches of your network. This new network could be just what you need to get you through trying times now or in the future.

Keep in mind, too, that gratitude has the power to hack the time-space continuum, to bring people who once meant a great deal to you back into your orbit. It reanimates once-meaningful connections and provides a reason to get back in touch.

Sara Algoe proposed that when we search deep for the moments in which others have given us benefits, we find partners worth thanking. She called it the Find-Remind-Bind Theory. Once you remember just how much someone meant to you, you can reach out to them and express your thanks. That action alone acts as a binding agent, strengthening your relationship.

As such, those weak ties may not stay weak for long.

# Gratitude Inquiry:

- *Reflection: Who in your life do you feel awkwardness expressing gratitude to? For what reason? Are you too close to the source, or has the relationship lay dormant too long?*

- *Reflection: At what point in your life have you experienced a "loose connection" coming back around to bless you in unexpected ways?*

- *Action: Make a list of 3-5 people who are currently distant or "weak ties" and reach out to them to express gratitude.*

- *Bonus Action: Consider inviting a group of weak ties to a dinner party and using our Signature Gratitude Question to create connection amongst the group. Who would you invite?*

# The Five Love Languages

*"We tend to speak our own love language, to express love to others in a language that would make us feel loved. But if it is not his/her primary love language, it will not mean to them what it would mean to us."*
– Gary Chapman

R eady to start giving gratitude? Great! But before you do, you must realize that *how* you give it matters a great deal. It is crucial to do it in the way that the recipient will best receive it.

In his book *The Five Love Languages*, Gary Chapman explains that there are five different ways in which people want to be shown love:

1. Words of Affirmation
2. Acts of Service
3. Receiving Gifts
4. Quality Time
5. Physical Touch

Now, I know these have been billed as "love languages," but love and gratitude are closely linked. As such, understanding the concept of love languages and why they matter can help us give gratitude more effectively. Just like love, gratitude must be given in a way that resonates with your audience.

To clarify this concept, let me tell you a story. My friend used to work at a wonderful company. She put in five hard years running different divisions of the operation. When she decided it was time to move on, the founder took it personally and berated her for her decision.

The days passed, and my friend's last day at the company arrived. She was hoping for some final, personal outreach—some acknowledgment of the time, energy, and effort she'd dedicated to the founder over the years. Nothing happened.

Eventually, the founder sent a necklace via courier. With it was a note. It read:

*Thank you. I now realize everything I could have done to keep you . . . You know, I somehow envisioned you running our little company one day.*

Now, that's an example of selfish gratitude. The letter was all about the sender and her disappointment. But the necklace was the sticking point.

Not only was it an impersonal gift—procured with just a click on a website—it didn't reflect my friend's love languages.

My friend's love languages—the kinds of acts that make her feel appreciated—are quality time and physical touch. A good-bye hug wouldn't have been as flashy, but she would have felt like her boss cared. It would have provided closure.

Have you ever given gratitude in a manner that the recipient didn't seem to receive well? In 2021, I gave a ton of gratitude to friends, including a very specific and thoughtful gift to a close friend.

I had wanted to show him how much he meant to me, so I hired an artist to capture his favorite life moments and etch them into an artifact. I had done it many times before with people, and I thought it was one of the most meaningful gifts I could give. Our team spent hours answering the artist's questions about my friend's life. I was so proud when we shipped it.

But days and weeks went by, and I heard nothing from him. I know he's an extremely busy man, but I was starting to fear I had put something on the artifact that rubbed him the wrong way. Then, it dawned on me.

Eventually, I reached out and asked him, "Hey buddy, in what language do you like to receive appreciation?"

"Quality time and acts of service," he said. "But Chris, let me guess what your favorite language is? Gifts."

I had sent him a physical object when my friend would have much preferred that I visit him so we could spend some quality time together, or, maybe help him volunteer at a local nonprofit.

That's when I realized that **not all gratitude given is gratitude heard**. We tend to show love and appreciation through our own preferred language and fail to express gratitude in the manner that resonates most with our recipient.

When we give gratitude in the language that feels best for us, it can actually come across as convenient, selfish, insincere, or lazy. Those gestures fall flat. Meanwhile, when we give gratitude in the recipient's love language, it feels authentic and empathetic, and is much more likely to be seen or heard.

Reading Gary Chapman's book will help you identify your own love language, but the key is to take the time to understand the love languages of the people to whom you want to give gratitude.

You can simply observe the languages to which they seem to respond best, or even ask them about their preferred love language. They may appreciate the latter gesture in and of itself!

We often help our clients survey their teams to identify individual love languages. That way, they can create a company log of how people like to receive gratitude, and make sure to give it in a manner that resonates.

Now, keep in mind, giving gratitude in the language that's best for the recipient doesn't mean that you won't feel good giving it if the format doesn't align with your preferred love language. Scientists believe that altruistic behavior releases endorphins in the brain, producing the positive feeling known as the "helper's high." So, you as the giver will benefit regardless of the format! It's yet another reason to get giving.

## Gratitude Inquiry:

- *Reflection: Have you experienced someone showing you love in a way that didn't land? Could that have something to do with a difference in love languages? How can you go back and acknowledge their original positive intent?*

- *Reflection: What is the love language that is most convenient for you to give, but others might not enjoy receiving?*

- *Action: Reach back out to a few people you've talked to over the course of this book and ask what languages of appreciation they like to receive.*

# Make It Inconvenient

*"We can complain because rose bushes have thorns,*
*or rejoice because thorns have roses."*
– Alphonse Karr

Here's an inconvenient truth: If you're giving gratitude in a manner that's most meaningful for the receiver, chances are, it's going to be inconvenient for you. And that's actually a very good thing. Why?

We can measure inconvenience in terms of effort. In this case, we're talking about the amount of effort it takes you to give gratitude.

In a world where we've been conditioned to seek the path of least resistance—whether that's making purchases with one click, sending an ecard with the push of a button, or returning that T-shirt we ordered without a second thought—effort means something.

We don't necessarily value the stuff that comes easy. The speed and frequency with which we can do certain actions strips them of their meaning—and their joy.

For example, if using Instacart means we don't have to pick up our meat from the local butcher shop every week, that convenience robs us of the opportunity to connect with that butcher store owner and build a relationship with her over time. If a podcast production agency takes away the burden of editing every episode ourselves, it also steals our opportunity to review everything we spoke and learned about—as well as the chance to fall in love with our brilliant guests. If a nonprofit makes it easy to donate money online, it takes away all that we gain from volunteering our time.

The same goes for gratitude. The internet is full of services that make sending a gift card online or connecting over video to express our thanks totally seamless. But in the process, we lose out on the opportunity to put in the time and effort to make our gratitude known—to write out words of appreciation and place them in the mailbox down the street, or fly across the country to celebrate a loved one who has done so much for us. Moreover, those are the gestures that register.

As Oliver Burkeman writes in *Four Thousand Weeks: Time Management for Mortals*, "smoothness and convenience is a dubious virtue, since it's often the unsmooth textures of life that make it liveable, helping nurture the relationships that are crucial for mental and physical health, and for the resilience of our communities."

He explains that when you rely too much on convenience, you end up becoming socially isolated. Technology induces loneliness, which has a greater net negative effect than not doing the task at all.

Why do I say gratitude should be inconvenient?

Well, gratitude should require effort.

How much effort?

We can look to a Cost-Benefit Appraisal to find out. There are three factors that determine whether the person to whom you're giving gratitude will see and feel what you're offering up.

First on the benefit appraisal is the value of what you're giving. Is it a physical gift, an act of service, or quality time—and do they want it? I'm not talking about the quantitative value of the item or service, I'm talking about the qualitative value to the recipient. It must be valuable to the person in order to mean something. For instance, if you are looking for a gift to a friend who has run many marathons, a book on training for one's first marathon probably wouldn't be very valuable to him. Meanwhile, while it would cost less in dollars, spending an early Saturday morning biking alongside him with coconut water and bananas as he preps for his next race could be an extremely meaningful gift.

Second, how much does it cost, or how inconvenient is it for you to give it? Are you buying a book on Amazon and shipping it to your mother in one fell, frictionless swoop, or are you driving the three hours it takes to get to her house in time for Sunday dinner?

It doesn't take much to give gratitude when it's convenient. But when it's inconvenient, you really have to want to give it, and that means something.

Third, to what extent do you *want* to give this gratitude? I call this genuine fucks given (sorry, Lynn). Do you actually want to show gratitude to this person, or are you being forced to do it out of some moral or social obligation? Waking up and biking alongside my friend during his marathon preparation is something I do because I genuinely want to support my friend. It's one small way of thanking him for how good he's been to me through the years. I have many, many fucks to give in his honor.

Each of these elements has a threshold, one that can only be determined by the recipient, and you have to surpass that threshold to ensure that your gratitude is seen and felt.

How do you know when you've crossed the threshold?

I wish there was a good way. But you don't have to worry about how your gratitude is received, or sit around waiting for them to respond with their own display of appreciation. When you give gratitude in ways inconvenient to you, the message will almost definitely come through. And your recipient is that much more likely to give that gratitude right back, or pay it forward in a generous way.

## Gratitude Inquiry:

- *Reflection: Where in your life do you value taking the easy route, rather than the route that requires tremendous effort?*

- *Reflection: How often do you express gratitude in a way that's most convenient for you? What is that go-to action for you?*

- *Action: Go out of your way to do something extremely inconvenient, yet positive, for another person this week. Write down the details you noticed in the journey along the way (ie: the horrible traffic, the smell of the subway, the silly dad jokes from the fish vendor).*

# Be a Good Receiver

*"Giving is virtuous, but so is accepting gifts gratefully."*
– Doe Zantamata

Regardless of your generation, you likely grew up being told that it is better to give, than to receive. The adage is an age-old attempt at preventing society from becoming overrun by narcissists and takers—people who are just out for themselves. Most of us have internalized this way of thinking, but it has its downsides.

If we spend all day just figuring out the next way to give or be of service, we are robbing ourselves of the ability to create real relationships and appreciate true connection—both of which require give *and* take.

Think about the last time someone tried to thank you. You may have felt self-conscious, and brushed it off or minimized your contribution with a quick "no problem," or something to that effect. But when we deflect, it only serves to make the giver perceive that we didn't feel the measure of their generosity in offering their gratitude. They miss out on the benefits that giving should make *them* feel, and feel less connected to us as a result.

But even when we know that it *is* important to receive, we still find it challenging.

Why?

Researcher Dr. John Amodeo has a few theories as to why receiving comes so hard for us. His first theory is that we have built up a defense against intimacy, because in a world that prioritizes surface-level relationships and instant connection, we actually fear it.

His second theory is all about control, and how much it hurts to let go of it. Dr. Amodeo points out that giving gratitude is a way of gaining control. Whether we give a physical gift, words of affirmation, or even our time, we're taking the narrative into our own hands. Meanwhile, we're hesitant to surrender that control by receiving others' appreciation.

Dr. Amodeo's third theory is that we fear there are strings attached to what we receive, and so we're hesitant to take anything from others—even their gratitude.

If you grew up in a home with parents who had high expectations, you're likely familiar with Dr. Amodeo's third theory. Maybe they wanted you to be the star football player on your team, or thc best chess player at your school, or go to the most illustrious college of all your friends.

They might have showered you with compliments and gifts to inspire you to achieve. But when you received their praise, you knew that there were expectations behind it. They weren't recognizing and encouraging you for being who you were, but rather for what you were doing—or what they wanted you to do, even if they believed their intentions were good. When gifts are tied to expectations, it's hard to receive them. It makes us jaded.

But we can counter the urge to reject others' expressions of gratitude, regardless of why we have it. All we have to do is accept what they're offering.

Seneca said, "When we have decided to accept, let us accept with cheerfulness, showing pleasure, and letting the giver see it, so that he may at once receive some return for his goodness. Let us therefore show how acceptable a gift is by loudly expressing our gratitude for it; and let us do so, not only in the hearing of the giver, but everywhere."

Think about that coworker who is always leaning in to compliment you on a job well done, or to spot you on a coffee run. Think about that friend who texts to thank you after a fun night out. What would happen if you just accepted their generosity, and acknowledged that it's their way of showing they care, rather than waiting for some other shoe to drop?

The next time someone gives you a compliment or offers up some gratitude, accept the benefit and rejoice. Stop deflecting. You deserve gratitude too—and they deserve to see you accept it.

## Gratitude Inquiry:

- *Reflection: What do you feel when you hear "it is better to give than receive?" Has this been true in your own life?*

- *Reflection: Where in our lives are we denying others of the joy of giving? Why might this be? (Reference Dr. John Amodeo's possible theories on page __ if you're having a hard time identifying why).*

- *Action: Think of someone who's offered you something lately - a gift, act of service, etc. Reach out to them and take them up on it this week!*

# You Get What You Observe

*"There are only two ways to live your life. One is as though nothing is a miracle. The other is as though everything is a miracle."*
– Albert Einstein

When it comes to gratitude, it's not just about how you give and receive; it's also about how you observe. Witnessing gratitude effectively can have a positive impact on all parties involved—giver, receiver, and observer—and ripple throughout a social network, improving well-being for everyone in the group. Talk about bang for your buck, particularly when times are tough!

Sara Algoe and her team conducted an excellent study on gratitude and the witnessing effect. They studied the impact of gratitude on numerous members of a group: a first-party giver (the grateful person), a second-party receiver (the benefactor), and a third-party witness (the observer).

They found that just observing the grateful person give gratitude to the benefactor inspired the observer to affiliate more closely with the grateful person—even though they didn't know them (in the study, observers simply watched videos of grateful people giving gratitude to benefactors).

At 7:47, we see similar scenarios play out every day, when we invite attendees to spend fifteen minutes in random, three-person breakout groups as part of our Virtual Gratitude Experience™.

In the breakout rooms, each person is given five minutes to share stories of gratitude as they talk about the people in their life whom they've never thought to thank. The grateful people are likely giving gratitude to individuals whom the others don't know and will probably never meet: mothers, teachers, dogs, even ex-spouses.

Just witnessing the grateful person makes those observers want to connect with them on a deeper level, even if they have never met the benefactor before. They perceive the grateful person to be warm, caring, generous, and inviting—and thus someone they want to know.

You can see it in their eyes. So often, the grateful person tears up when they tell their story, and so does the observer—just from having heard it. The effects are lasting too: Time and time again, those who have met in breakout groups and heard each others' gratitude stories have become friends, or even romantic partners!

My friend Diana Elaine Miller shared a powerful account of how meaningful observing gratitude can be.

Diana is of Tamil descent. In Tamil culture, there is no word for gratitude. Instead, people show gratitude through ritual chanting, praising and touching the feet of their elders, lowering or averting their eyes, using honorable titles, changing their body posture, and changing their tone of voice.

Recently, Diana went to a family member's wedding and something miraculous occurred. When it was time for her to say "hello" to her grandmother, she did the only thing she could think of: she knelt down and kissed her grandmother's feet. It was her way of honoring and showing gratitude to her elders.

While she benefited from giving that gratitude and her grandmother benefited from receiving it, everyone else in the room—all those observers—felt the effects of their exchange.

When Diana looked up, many of her family members were crying just from witnessing her gratitude. They weren't the giver or the receiver, but they benefited just the same. And afterward, a number of cousins approached Diana, overwhelmed with emotion.

Algoe's study revealed another interesting insight. Observers not only had a high opinion of the grateful person after witnessing the interaction; they also thought more of the benefactor. They figured that, if the benefactor was receiving gratitude in the first place, they must be someone who had gone out of their way to do something wonderful for the grateful person. As such, they wanted to connect with the benefactor too.

We've seen this happen again and again as well. When we ask teams at our Virtual Gratitude Experiences™ to practice peer-to-peer gratitude, those in attendance share that they want a closer relationship with the benefactor too.

Finally, observing all this gratitude inspires us to become better people ourselves, and to perform more grateful actions as a means of doing so.

Social psychologist Jonathan Haidt describes the emotions created in these situations as those of "elevation." He explains that "elevation increases the likelihood that a witness to good deeds will soon become a doer of good deeds, then elevation sets up the possibility for the same sort of 'upward spiral' in a group. This socioemotional cycle centered on gratitude could continue forever."

It's amazing what taking the time to observe can do! When you see someone giving gratitude to another, approach that person and introduce yourself to them. Thank them for taking the time to thank others. They will be floored by it! Conversely, when you see someone receiving gratitude from another person, go up to the benefactor and ask them what caused them to provide the benefit in the first place. Ask them how they learned to be so good and giving. It's elevation in motion.

## Gratitude Inquiry:

- *Reflection: What have you learned from watching others express gratitude for others? Does their language of appreciation look different than what you're used to?*

- *Reflection: Referencing Sara Algoe's "witnessing effect," when's the last time you befriended a person because you witnessed them giving gratitude to others, or watched them receive gratitude from others?*

- *Action: Observe the people around you this week and acknowledge when you see someone giving gratitude for another. Watch the ripple effect and enjoy the elevation!*

# Great Leaders are Grateful

*"Gratitude turns what we have into enough, and more.
It turns denial into acceptance, chaos into order,
confusion into clarity . . . it makes sense of our past, brings peace
for today, and creates a vision for tomorrow."*
– Melody Beattie

# Grateful Leaders Listen

*"Listening is the doorway to understanding;*
*it's very difficult to inspire people if you're not*
*speaking appropriately to them."*
– Julian Treasure

The pandemic had been raging for several months when we wrapped up a Virtual Gratitude Experience™ with Lisa and Meaghan, the leaders of a very large team at a Fortune 50 company. When we came to the end of the ninety-minute session, we handed the microphone over to Meaghan to close things out.

"The beauty of leading this team is that I get to hear a lot about what you all are going through," she said. "Today, many of you told really hard stories, and my heart goes out to everyone struggling right now. We heard happy stories too, and we can tap into each other's pain and happiness to create empathy and connection. I am very proud of all of you for your courage and willingness to share. And the fact that we can do this in such a big company is a really beautiful thing. So, thank you to each of you."

As leaders, Meaghan and Lisa's decision to say yes to our session was the first step in reaping the benefits of gratitude for their team. But listening to their colleagues' stories with empathy was the next one.

To give gratitude that is authentic, specific, and in the language of the recipient, you must pay attention to those you serve. Leaders who fail to adopt a posture of otherness, who aren't curious about what makes those around them tick, fall into the trap of egocentric bias. Those with egocentric bias prioritize their perspective over others', or buy into their own hype—adopting a higher opinion of oneself than is actually warranted.

Egocentric bias is a hindrance to your potential. Meanwhile, when you are open to others' insights, you embrace the opportunity to change for the better, and enable others to feel validated as they help find a solution.

Six-time Stanley Cup champion, and one of the greatest influences in my life, Mark Messier attributes much of his leadership style to empathy, curiosity, and the ability to listen to others' insights. In his book, *No One Wins Alone*, he describes the most effective form of leadership is one that is absent of ego, and that a good leader need only have one thought in mind: the collective.

After a perspective-shifting trip to Barbados early in his hockey career, he made a commitment to appreciate the diversity of human beings, acknowledging that people not only act in different ways, but think in ways different than he'd ever imagined. As he writes, "Just because I wasn't familiar with someone else's perspective didn't make them wrong. Never again would I believethat someone was fundamentally mistaken because their mind worked in a way I was unfamiliar with. I saw that they could just be exploring different parts of this same huge landscape of possibility."

Mark's ability to grasp this concept helped him transform into the person he would become: a curious and empathetic individual who would grow to become one of the all-time greatest leaders in sports.

To be a great leader in any field, you must first show people that you appreciate their input. Unfortunately, we can't expect others to simply pick up on the gratitude that radiates from us. We need to express it regularly and in a way that's meaningful to *them*. As we explored when we discussed the five love languages, some people like plaques, others appreciate a pat on the back. Some won't feel seen unless you share words of encouragement. But you won't know what resonates until you ask.

Leaders who take the time to listen to what their teams want and need and show gratitude accordingly create an environment where everyone feels heard, and is thus inspired to give back.

As Mark says at the end of his book, "With respect and gratitude, I say: thank you, thank you, thank you!" My hope is that his words of gratitude shine bright for all to see and pay forward.

## Gratitude Inquiry:

- *Reflection: As a leader, when was the last time you carved meaningful time on your calendar just to sit and listen uninterrupted to your team? What did you learn from them?*

- *Reflection: What gets in the way of taking time to slow down and listen to others?*

- *Action: This week, reach out to someone who contributes meaningful input into your life and schedule a time to ask them deep, open-ended questions about their life story.*

# Lead with a Question

*"It is easier to judge the mind of a man*
*by his questions rather than his answers."*
– Voltaire

Think back on the leaders who made the greatest impact on your life. Do they stand out because they were interesting, or because they took a genuine interest in you? Did those people seem to have all the answers, or did they admit that they still had so much to learn and appreciate?

In most cases, it's the curious people who make their mark on our worlds. And one way to tap into that curiosity is through gratitude.

How do you express your gratitude when you've just met someone?

Lead with a question.

Questions help you get deeper faster—all while showing your appreciation for a new colleague's knowledge and experience. For example, if someone is considering the inherent risk of taking on a new role, they want leaders who will listen with empathy, and give them their undivided attention. Show them you care with questions, and don't be afraid to go deep.

It can be easy to lean on small talk, especially if you feel nervous or uncomfortable. But that won't produce the same kind of connection, or elicit nearly as much vulnerability. We've all been to events where we've been tasked with meeting new people. They were likely filled with surface-level inquiries like "How are you enjoying the weather?" "How did you like the coffee at the buffet?" With questions like these, you can talk about nothing forever.

But what does that actually achieve? Nothing. To others, you're just a business card from a conference where they randomly heard Sheryl Crow sing at the after party (no offense to Sheryl; she's still rocking).

Imagine if you did something different. Imagine if you gave them the gift of your full attention, your great questions, and a radically safe space. In a world where so many of us are lonely, disconnected, or unfulfilled, your presence might just save their life.

At the heart of my life's work are questions that I began to ask because—quite frankly—I was lonely. Yes, I have a true talent for connecting people, but as a result, I can easily fade into the background. If you are the connector, the hinge, the broker, the bridge between social networks, it's easy to feel invisible. You're the doorman. Everybody knows your name and face, but they don't know who you truly are.

I spent so much time feeling as if I were standing at the edge of the circle, like my invitation was always lost in the mail, and it followed me from childhood through my darkest chapters. Depression. Suicide attempts. Rehab.

Then, I stumbled onto the power of questions, and that changed everything. The insecurity of being excluded and the pain of feeling unheard inspired me to create the kind of experience where I wouldn't have to struggle to fit in. I could make myself valuable by serving others.

I could create gatherings where people felt safe to share. Where people felt heard, and like their stories mattered. Hosting experiences with this aim meant focusing less on designing the perfect ambiance and more on the question at the heart of the experience.

Your goal in entering into any conversation should be to create the kind of space where another person feels heard. This is where you can build and develop an authentic connection—something for which both of you can be grateful.

When you become genuinely curious about others, you stop seeking out small talk. You start going deeper, and you learn how to truly listen. When you listen with gratitude, you aren't distracted with the work of formulating a response, because you don't need to have the answers. You're poised to learn instead of judge. And when someone trusts you enough to share vulnerably, you have the grace to feel honored by that trust.

So, take a deep breath, acknowledge any emotions that may be holding you back, and give gratitude for the person in front of you by asking a deeper question.

According to Sir Francis Bacon, "A good prudent question is one-half of wisdom." I'd say a good, prudent question is one-half of gratitude!

# Gratitude Inquiry:

- *Reflection: Think back on the leaders who made the greatest impact on your life. Do they stand out because they were interesting, or because they took a genuine interest in you?*

- *Reflection: What are some of the best thought-provoking questions you've been asked throughout your life?*

- *Action: Write down a few open-ended questions you could ask the next time you find yourself with a brand new person. Consider jotting these questions on a note in your phone so you have them handy when the time comes.*

# Achieve the Golden Mean



*If you could give credit or thanks to one person in your life, that you don't give enough credit or thanks to, who would that be?*

People are surprised that our Signature Gratitude Question stirs up so many different types of emotions, from guilt, shame, and regret, to happiness, connectedness, and joy.

Why is it so evocative?

The question achieves what Aristotle described as the Golden Mean: the midpoint between the extremes of excess and deficiency.

The question isn't too easy, like *What are you grateful for?* It's not too hard like, *What's the meaning of life?* Instead it lies smack dab in the middle, giving people the wiggle room to think and come up with something meaningful without getting overwhelmed.

This gratitude question opens the door to connection in a non-threatening way, whether you're answering it alone or with other people. You're recalling a story about someone else, rather than sharing vulnerably about yourself. And because it feels like it's about *them*, you're more likely to act.

When you recover lost memories or connections with people you never thought to thank, you are presented with the opportunity to reconnect.

Start by practicing this question for yourself and taking action to thank the people in your life who you have never thought to thank. Then consider how you can help others find gratitude for the people in *their* lives by facilitating a conversation.

Note, too, that our question isn't the be-all, end-all. No question is.

Asking insightful questions isn't about sounding smart. You're opening a door, not setting a trap. Before you enter a gratitude conversation, check your own motivation. Ask yourself why you're embarking on that particular discussion. Is this purposeful? Are you genuinely curious about this individual? What are you open to learning when you seek their point of view? What are you hoping to facilitate for them?

Is your question stimulating? Most people approach gratitude by asking the easy one: *What are you grateful for?* This canned question elicits a canned response. You'll hear the surface-level, tip-of-the-tongue stuff:

"I'm grateful for the ability to go on a bike ride this weekend in beautiful weather."

"I'm grateful for this new watch that lets me see how many steps I've taken and how many hours of deep sleep I've had."

"I'm grateful for my dog."

If you want to stay in the small talk territory, there's nothing wrong with this approach. But if you want to forge a deeper connection, you need to go deeper.

When you start asking better questions, you will start to hear "I've never thought about that."

Give your partner permission to pause. Reflection is critical for meaningful gratitude. A great answer to a good question isn't necessarily on the tip of their tongue. Making space means making peace with silence.

Tim Ferriss once explained, "The people who are the very best at this are the ones who hear my question and respond with: 'You're asking the wrong question. The better question is . . .'"

## Gratitude Inquiry:

- *Reflection: What type of questions do you ask when you're not actually motivated or interested in the conversation? How does that type of conversation make you feel?*


- *Reflection: Think back to a time when someone asked you a question that you weren't interested in answering and complete this sentence – "you're asking the wrong question, the better question is: ______"*


- *Action: Write down six types of stories and information you actually want to know and learn from others. Let these curiosities be a guide to the questions you ask moving forward.*

# Listen Actively



How do you get your people to go deep as a leader—or anyone else, for that matter?

Your ability to go deeper relies on your ability to listen and to ask questions. Use active listening techniques to help them open up further. Maya Angelou said it best: If you make your partner feel safe, seen and heard, they will remember that attention forever. And they'll deliver as a result.

Our friend Chris Voss wrote a wonderful book about the power of empathy in conversation. It's called *Never Split the Difference: Negotiating As If Your Life Depended On It*. Chris started his career as a cop. From there he moved to the FBI, where he worked in the hostage negotiation division. But soon after he arrived, he realized they were doing it all wrong.

FBI agents were using logic to navigate a hostage scene. But Chris realized that people don't commit crimes and take hostages out of logic; they do it because they are driven by emotion. He surmised that if negotiators could empathize with hostage-takers, they would feel seen and heard, and reveal something that could help the negotiators deescalate the situation. So, he decided to create an entire program to train negotiators on how to negotiate with empathy.

Voss writes, "This tactical empathy is not about manipulation, it's about connection. Just because it's a good strategy in negotiation does not make it insincere. The desire to be understood is a basic human need. Your relationships will thrive the more you learn how to be empathetic"

In the world outside of hostage negotiation, we can use these same principles to make those with whom we're conversing with feel seen and heard. Conveying empathy through question-asking is the greatest form of gratitude I think humans can muster—especially when others are going through hard times. Listening with empathy helps diffuse the anger and anxiety that people feel.

To do it effectively, start with some reflection. People want reassurance that they have been heard. Thus, you shouldn't just react or judge. Invented by Voss, mirroring is simply when you repeat one, two, or three words from the last words your counterpart has spoken. This helps let them know they came through loud and clear.

Sometimes in our experiences, people give credit and thanks to those who have hurt them in some way—a great choice, since processing trauma through gratitude can be incredibly powerful. But it can be difficult to know how to respond.

Repeating—or mirroring—and then labeling emotions can help.

Why?

Mirroring lets people know that you heard them. Labeling emotions helps to normalize them, the value of which cannot be overstated—particularly in a society that struggles to validate emotion.

Say someone gives thanks to a mother who never said "I love you." You can start by mirroring. You might say, "Your mom never told you she loved you?" That's just me repeating what I just heard from them. They will likely say, "correct." They'll probably elaborate on what they just shared.

Then, label that emotional response. "It sounds like that was painful." This is a sample tactic. You use labeling phrases like, "it sounds like, seems like, looks like" to help the other person feel like you understand them. Keep in mind that you're not jumping in with your story; you're just helping them tell parts of theirs.

Finally, close out their story with gratitude for their vulnerability. You could say something like, "I just want to acknowledge that I can't make this pain go away, but your willingness to share gave us the opportunity to connect on a deeper level. Thank you."

We always say that the greatest present you can give is your presence. You practicing these active listening techniques will be life changing to some. Don't be surprised if they give some gratitude in return. It's rare and remarkable to feel heard, and it all starts with the right questions!

# Gratitude Inquiry:

- *Reflection: When's the last time you listened in order to ask your next question, rather than listened just so you could tell your story next?*

- *Reflection: When have you struggled to go "deep" with others? Reflect on what is and isn't working about your approach.*

- *Action: Set a goal to use "it sounds like, it seems like, it looks like" at least five times in your next conversation with a friend.*

# Found When the World Is Down

*"Always hold fast to the present. Every situation, indeed every moment, is of infinite value, for it is the representative of a whole eternity."*
– Johann Wolfgang von Goethe

Did you know that when the world is down in the dumps, or going through hard times, you may be most prone to achieve?

It was in the darkest of holes that some of the world's most successful companies were born. In his book *The Obstacle Is the Way: The Timeless Art of Turning Trials into Triumph*, Ryan Holiday writes that some of the largest companies in the world were actually founded in the midst of turbulent times.

FedEx, UPS, Walt Disney, Hewlett Packard, Costco, General Motors, LinkedIn, and Microsoft were all started in periods of recession. Their founders weren't worried about what the world would be like when the economy bounced back. They weren't overwhelmed with questions about what things would look like fifty years down the line—all that mattered was right then. They focused on solving the problem at hand, in a manner that aligned with the current state of things. We all know what happened next.

Gratitude can help you stay present and avoid the anxiety of looking too far into the future, even when the present is plagued with issues. It can help you muster the moral courage necessary to take that first step when the going is already tough.

Don't wait for things to be just right to make your next big move. Be grateful for everything that's brought you to this point and begin now. Growth and innovation can occur through crises.

Take, for instance, Jill Shipp, Chief Business Development Officer of Hospitality Health ER. I met Jill and her team in Nashville while on a trip with Andy Ellwood and his friends. Prior to COVID, she and her mother were running a successful medical practice with a few locations in Texas.

Jill's mother had started the company as a single mom with four kids and no education. Against all odds, Jill's mother put herself through nursing school while working multiple jobs, taking care of her own mother, and more. It took fifteen years, but eventually their company became an industry leader in a male-dominated industry.

And then COVID hit, and with it came extreme challenges that no one in medicine knew quite how to address. Jill's practices began to fill up with deathly ill patients. Worse, they had no way of helping them and nowhere to send them.

So with nothing to lose, they created something brand new. To treat the influx of COVID patients, they set up a tent city in their parking lots, complete with AC and heat, water stations, and bathrooms. They treated patients with regular emergencies inside with one team, while another dedicated group responded to the COVID group—fully outfitted in personal protective equipment (PPE). They worked in 100 degree heat and through rain and snow storms, caring for ICU-style patients with very few resources.

As the demand grew, they adapted, purchasing an empty clinic and a bank blocks away from their busiest location and transforming them into makeshift ICU units within weeks.

The ancillary staff joined their efforts, leaving their admin and marketing posts to pitch in in the ER when the medical staff became overwhelmed.

Everyone worked sick and scared for over a year. But they also found gratitude and achieved growth.

I asked Jill what she learned during that difficult period. She said, "It taught me so much about going for it when no one else has the guts. I learned that with a strong, thoughtful leader, a team can accomplish more than what feels possible. I learned about coping with the long haul of trauma while still being in the depths of the storm. I learned a lot about the human spirit both with our staff and patients."

She said that she actually didn't realize how grateful she was in the moment—that clarity came after some of the storm had passed. "Gratitude is often veiled by focus, strength of spirit, and a sense of camaraderie. And a sense of humor regardless of the difficulty," she explained. It took her a long time to feel grateful. What helped was stepping back to see the life-changing impact she and her team were making.

Now that we're on the other side of the pandemic, Jill can focus on growth—not just out of necessity, but also out of desire. Jill and her team have big plans for location expansion and even growing the services they offer.

Was running a business during a pandemic and economic downturn difficult for Jill and her team?

Yes.

Did it give her the benefits of resilience, community closeness, new perspectives, and new opportunities?

Also yes.

She is forever grateful for the lessons she learned during such a difficult time. The hope, pride, optimism, and self-confidence she developed during that period of adversity has set her company up to make a tremendous impact for many years to come. The life lessons you learn through plagues, pandemics, and wars can provide a window of opportunity amidst crisis. When the dust finally settles, take the time to be grateful.

## Gratitude Inquiry:

- *Reflection: What types of new opportunities do you see around yourself right now because the world is going through hard times?*

- *Reflection: What parts of your character and personality shine when the going gets tough? Is it your humor, problem-solving skills, collaborative spirit, etc.?*

- *Action: Choose one person in your extended community who is going through a tough time right now and express gratitude for the courageous ways they're showing up to the situation.*

# Enjoy the Spectacle of Failure

*"Even so a fire masters that which is cast upon it,
and though a small flame would have been extinguished,
your great blaze quickly makes the added fuel its own,
consumes it, and grows mightier therefrom."*
– Marcus Aurelius

It was early evening on December 10, 1914. A fire had broken out at Thomas Edison's plant, and he and his son, Charles, watched as ten of the buildings went up in flames—along with numerous patents, blueprints, inventions. Between six and eight fire departments rushed to a blaze that was ultimately too large to control.

Edison told Charles, "Go get your mother and all her friends. They'll never see a fire like this again." When Charles protested, Edison calmly replied "It's all right. We've just got rid of a lot of rubbish."

At the peak of what was thought to be the height of his inventive genius, Edison lost more than half of his buildings to an unforeseen tragedy. Eventually, he would estimate that $900,000 worth of buildings, inventions, and more were torched—about $23 million in today's dollars). And that doesn't account for the inestimable potential of the prototypes and the records that were lost.

He could have resorted to anger, resentment, blame, regret, or depression, but he didn't. He could have quit, but he didn't. Instead, Edison instructed his son to get his mother and his friends so they wouldn't miss the spectacle.

Later that night, he said, "Although I am over sixty-seven years old, I'll start all over again tomorrow." And he did.

In less than a month—with double shifts, a generous loan from Henry Ford, and a healthy dose of enthusiasm—Edison and his team were back in business. They would go on to make nearly $10 million the following year.

Edison was successful not only because he had mastered his emotions, but also because he modeled resilience for his team. There was only one thing to do after the flames died down: jump back in and rebuild.

Years later, he would give immense gratitude to that setback, crediting it for clearing a path to even greater success.

Giving gratitude to your failures fosters a growth mindset. That growth mindset allows you to recover and move forward faster.

Unsure of how to default to gratitude instead of disappointment in the face of failure? You often need to achieve some degree of removal from the situation (gratefully processing the past is a lot easier than gratefully processing a moment in which the steaming pile of shit is still within smelling distance, to be frank).

But that doesn't mean you have to wait. Instead, you can use your imagination. Picture your much older self. You're finally where you always hoped you'd be. Now, approach your failure from that place, seeing it through the eyes of someone who has moved on from it.

# Gratitude Inquiry:

- *Reflection: When have disappointments and failures overwhelmed you in the past?*


- *Reflection: Like Thomas Edison, have you seen others successfully process disappointments and failures through gratitude?*


- *Action: Picture your much older self. You've reached a place where you always hoped you'd be. Now, think about a disappointment or failure that you're currently dealing with. How would it feel to approach that situation from the place of seeing it through the eyes of someone who has moved on? What opportunities might that failure have opened up for you?*

# Be a Grateful Owner

*"As we express our gratitude, we must never forget that the highest appreciation is not to utter words but to live by them."*
– John F. Kennedy

Osteria Francescana in Modena, Italy, is a three-Michelin-star, high-end dining experience. It was named the world's best restaurant in 2016 and 2018. I had the tremendous honor of securing a reservation at the request of my dear friend Michele Buster. I knew, going in, that it would be a dining experience that would change my life.

Upon arrival, the waitstaff greeted me and my father with a glass of champagne and open arms, and over the next twelve courses, they became like family—sharing stories of the old country and getting to know us in intimate detail.

About halfway through dinner, I felt my jaw drop. My culinary hero, owner and chef Massimo Bottura, showed up to our table. He had come to hear our story. He asked good questions, listened with empathy, and when he left to get back to the kitchen, I felt that he understood my soul.

By joining us tableside, he allowed us to give him gratitude, and offered it in return—and the restaurant's patrons observed our compassionate interaction.

While the food was extraordinary, it was my gratitude exchange with Massimo that stuck with me. Joining us for ten minutes of his time cost Massimo no money, but it was an incredibly impactful investment. I came away moved by the experience not because of the food, but because of how Massimo made me feel in just a fraction of my time there.

Massimo's personal touch and the moment of gratitude we shared is market differentiation in action. His business thrives on gratitude, compassion, empathy, and trust. He and his team value connection over profit and honesty over everything—and it shows.

If you want to make a lasting impact, consider the ways in which you can give our customers a personal moment of thanks. It's truly priceless.

## Gratitude Inquiry:

- *Reflection: Have you had an experience of a "Massimo" in your life, an owner who took time to show you he cared? How did that impact your experience?*


- *Reflection: What type of meaningful moments do the people around you value? How can you show up for them during those times?*

- *Action: Put yourself in the shoes of a customer, client, or teammate. Commit to one easy way you can express gratitude for their investment in you or your business this week.*

# Empower People, Inspire Consciousness

*"A thankful heart is not only the greatest virtue,*
*but the parent of all the other virtues."*
– Cicero

My friend Dwayne J. Clark has a mission: to empower people and inspire consciousness through gratitude.

Dwayne was the youngest of four children, raised by a loving single mother near the wheat fields of Eastern Washington. His mom worked long, hard hours as a line cook, but it wasn't always enough to make ends meet or keep food on the table. At one point, his mother stole several potatoes from the restaurant where she worked—vowing to replace them—and made potato soup to feed the family, which Dwayne and his siblings ate for many days.

But his mother didn't let her struggles get her down. She used to tell him, "When bad things happen, learn from the pain. Don't let that vivid feeling be lost. There is learning to be had in what just happened to you—something that will elevate you beyond where you were before. That's how the human spirit evolves! No matter what you do," she went on, "Don't ever forget where you came from, and that you once had to eat potato soup every day. When you have employees, be there for them, and they will always be there for you."

Dwayne held tight to those words, and continues to live them today. He believes that the universe creates deep dark holes for us to journey into, ways for us to bottom out, so that we have a real appreciation for the times in which we are walking among the clouds. In short, you have to experience pain to fully embrace pleasure. When you're in the hole, you don't have to stay long, but you do have to recognize what that time is teaching you.

He never forgot what his mother said. Over the years, Dwayne built an empire with thousands of employees. His company is often considered one of the best organizations to work for in America. He also supports more than seventy local and global charities and has founded four of his own including the Potato Soup Foundation, the Queen Bee Café, the D1 Foundation, and the Clark Family Foundation.

Every year, Dwayne produces his annual EPIC conference. The acronym stands for Empowering People Inspiring Consciousness. It's one of the most important investments he makes in his team and company's culture. But sales goals, department reporting, and employee reviews are not on the agenda. Instead, the primary task is to focus on one's self-awareness, consciousness, and dreams. It's a way to "hit the pause button on life" and explore what really matters.

The theme of the 2021 conference was gratitude. It was three days of the world's best speakers coming together to share their thoughts on gratitude, from Whoopi Goldberg, to Amal Clooney, Abby Wambach, and so many others. The day was filled with gratitude exercises, experiences, learning opportunities and more.

Together, the team took a moment to reflect on where they came from to gain the inspiration and energy necessary to innovate in a tough market in 2022. The event was a resounding success and, as happens every year, his team walked away feeling seen and heard by Dwayne, and ready to tackle any obstacles that would appear in the year to come.

Your struggle may have looked different from Dwayne's. You may not have grown up eating potato soup for days on end, or working to find your way out of rural Washington. But we all have struggles that we can draw on in life. We've all been through something that we shouldn't forget if we want to build something better for those in our charge.

## Gratitude Inquiry:

- *Reflection: What does it feel like when you are empowered? What actions would you take in that state that you otherwise wouldn't?*


- *Reflection: As Dwayne's mom said, "When bad things happen, learn from the pain. Don't let that vivid feeling be lost." What negative situations like potato poverty will you carry with you as part of your story?*

- *Action: Make a list of three people who's inspiring stories you can share with your immediate community.*

# Prioritize Connection

*"Loneliness is proof that your innate search*
*for connection is intact."*
– Martha Beck

Emotional and mental health issues are on the rise, and for many of us, work only contributes to the struggle. After two years of isolation and remote working, employees are ill-equipped to deal with greater levels of anxiety and depression. And their leadership hasn't done enough to help.

Why would we? We haven't been taught to think about our responsibility to support our people in that manner.

For the longest time, society has built the workplace into a rigid space devoid of humanity. But thanks to the disruption caused by the pandemic, business leaders have been forced to have a conversation about addressing personal needs and professional demands in a real way.

Employees are no longer willing to separate the person they are at home from the one who arrives at work, because work from home has become the new normal. And when people began commuting from their bedrooms to kitchens, living rooms, and home offices, the reality that they carry their stress and anxiety into their work and vice versa became even harder to avoid. It's up to leaders to help alleviate that. Gratitude can be an important tool to do so.

Gratitude creates positive emotions, which can become contagious within organizations. Studies have shown that a leader's positive emotions often predict the performance of the entire group. Further, as *Forbes* Human Resources Councilmember Kelly Siegel notes, "a culture of gratitude . . . can drive productivity, employee retention, wellness and engagement. Instituting gratitude at work is something anyone can do, from front-line team members to the CEO. Gratitude is viral, so once people see appreciation catching on, they are likely to jump in and keep it going."

If gratitude isn't at the center of your operations, it's time to change that. People are in search of a sense of community and belonging—some of our most basic needs—now more than ever. Work can be the place that they find it, and it can happen through gratitude. But that doesn't mean it will be easy.

Even for the most forward-thinking organizations, weaving authenticity and connection into company culture—the kind of culture that makes people feel grateful—is no effortless task. At a recent Virtual Gratitude Experience™, an employee emerged from a breakout group and said, "You know what I learned? We all want to put our best face forward when we come to work. But we're all dealing with our issues—our own strengths and weaknesses. We all have a story. It's interesting to take our fake face off and bring our real face out."

I watched everyone nod in unison.

Despite being part of a company that actively invests in their employees' well-being, it was clear that people were still craving meaningful conversation and connection with one another. They wanted a chance to be real with their colleagues, an important opportunity since many of us spend more time communicating with them than our friends or family.

Prioritizing connection is not a one-time gig. It takes consistent effort, practice, and repetition. You can start with the kinds of conversations you promote.

During the pandemic, we have seen people talk about tough topics more readily, from workplace conditions to political issues. Many employers find it hard to handle uncomfortable topics, but embracing them is the way to go.

Inviting in tough topics of discussion creates a sense of belonging in the office, and makes room for gratitude. If you are willing to welcome uncomfortable conversations, you will likely find that employees are more prepared to open up and talk about their fears. And you'll find, too, that they're grateful for the space to do so.

## Gratitude Inquiry:

- *Reflection: What parts of the workplace around you have become a rigid space devoid of humanity?*

- *Reflection: What's the most inspiring "real" conversation you've had with your team or leadership? What kind of trust and connection did that build between the two of you?*

- *Action: Write down one tough or uncomfortable conversation you know you need to have at work. Write about how you can use gratitude in that conversation to build connection.*

# Employ Gratitude to Build Teams

*"Every goal I've ever scored belonged to my entire team.*
*When you score, you better start pointing.*
*When a member of the Pack scores, there are only*
*two options: We're either rushing or we're pointing."*
– Abby Wambach

Watch videos of Abby Wambach, the world's former leading goal-scorer, celebrate, and you'll notice a curious habit. Each time she puts one between the posts, the two-time Olympic Gold Medalist & FIFA World Cup Champion points to the teammate who passed her the ball. It's a signal to everyone watching that the teammate is partially responsible for her success.

At Dwayne's aforementioned conference, we heard Wambach share with the audience that she could do what she did only because of the Wolfpack of players who passed her the ball when she was in the scoring position.

Like Wambach, researcher Francesca Gino knows that by thanking your team, those team members "experience stronger feelings of self-efficacy and social worth, motivating them to engage in prosocial behavior," and we got to see it play out on the field.

Leaders can apply that lesson to the workplace, finding ways to make connections with those at every level of the organization through gratitude.

What you appreciate, appreciates: when you recognize someone's unique qualities or contributions, you'll see them blossom before your eyes—meeting and exceeding your expectations as they fulfill their potential.

While conducting research for his book *Leading with Gratitude*, our friend Chester Elton found that, during exit interviews, the number one reason people give as to why they are leaving a company is that they don't feel appreciated by their manager.

If you want to make gratitude part of your company culture, both you and your team must practice it on a regular basis. A great place to start is by helping your employees appreciate the people with whom they work. One simple way to practice gratitude is to allocate time each quarter for employees to write thank-you notes to their coworkers.

When you make a point of pointing to your team, everyone feels the love, and they'll perform better as a result.

## Gratitude Inquiry:

- *Reflection: Have you experienced feeling unappreciated by a manager before? How did that impact your daily experience at work?*

- *Reflection: What's one thing you would love to be appreciated for by your team right now? How would that recognition support you moving forward?*


- *Action: Pick one person on your team to reach out and share gratitude with this week.*

# Uncover Common Core Values

*"The art of learning fundamental common
values is perhaps the greatest gain of travel to those
who wish to live at ease among their fellows"*
– Freya Stark

Want a foolproof strategy for cultivating a genuine sense of belonging?

I've got an exercise that can help. It involves capturing your values, and those of the people around you.

Toward the end of some of our Virtual Gratitude Experiences™, we get people to capture values as a way to build bridges and move forward. After spending much of the experience helping each other give credit and thanks to members of the team whom they had never thought to thank, we ask them to take out a piece of paper and write down three more people on their team whom they had never thought to thank.

Then, under each person's name, we ask them to write a paragraph about that person. We prompt them with the following questions:

*What have you learned from them?*
*How did they help you on a particularly difficult project?*
*What did they learn from you?*

*What's the worst thing that ever happened to them?*

*How did they help you?*

Try to recall the emotion you felt when they provided this particular value to you, think about what it made you feel. Where does this feeling live in your body?

After that, we ask them to write down five to seven values that each of those people stands for. Then, we ask them to look for any commonalities between those values and their own. They might find overlaps like love, loyalty, honesty, or a myriad of other qualities.

Now, it's time to flip the script. We ask them to consider how those values show up in their lives today.

We ask them, *What stories do you tell yourself around those values?*

Why do we ask that last question?

The stories they tell help them communicate to the people on their team how much they relate to them. Stanford psychologist Kelly McGonigal describes the impact this way: "Writing about personal values makes people feel more powerful, in control, proud and strong. It also makes them feel more loving, connected, and empathetic toward others. It increases pain tolerance, enhances self-control, and reduces unhelpful rumination after a stressful experience."

The exercise has the potential to affect not just how you move forward from that moment, but also how you interact with and lead others. You'll realize you have a lot more in common with the people around you than you have differences. You'll feel a greater sense of connection, and the world will seem to be a much smaller place.

When you can connect gratitude and core values, you can start thinking big-picture and transform your outlook as an individual and as an organization.

## Gratitude Inquiry:

- *Reflection: What are your current core values?*

- *Reflection: Are those values in alignment with the values of the company you work for?*

- *Action: Take the person on your team who you gave gratitude to in the previous section, and write down 5-7 values that this person stands for. Do you find you have any values in common?*

# Drive Loyalty and Retention



If you're looking for an intervention that takes little time, improves individual employee well-being, deepens customer loyalty, and boosts your bottom line, look no further than gratitude.

As customer-retention expert Joey Coleman writes in his book, *Never Lose a Customer Again*, the process of advertising and marketing to new customers is far more expensive than the cost of any loyalty program that aims to keep current customers spending. And yet, the average business spends 6.9 percent of total revenue on marketing, and less than one fifth on customer retention.

Meanwhile, most companies see between 20 percent and 70 percent of those new customers disappear in less than 100 days. They break contracts, cancel memberships, stop using the product, and never come back. All that time and money invested in attracting them is lost.

It's not just lost customers that are costing you. According to Gallup, US businesses are losing $1 trillion every year due to voluntary employee turnover. In 2017, the Bureau of Labor Statistics estimated the annual overall employee turnover rate in the US was 26.3 percent. In the post-pandemic "Great Resignation," things are looking even worse. With that in mind, when you weigh the cost of investing in employee engagement against that of replacing an individual employee (from one-half to two times that employee's annual salary), the dollars speak for themselves.

And with studies pointing to a direct correlation between an employee's perception of being valued in the workplace and employee retention, and three out of four employees who don't feel their contributions are valued are actively applying elsewhere, it's time to consider how you communicate about value.

Gratitude can be the cornerstone of your retention plan for both customers and employees, the differentiating factor between your company and the competition.

Let's talk about customers first. Leaders often think that the best way to keep customers is to give them something. So, at the end of a calendar year, they send out the same old gift package with their company's name on it. Well, let me fill you in on a little secret: it's not nearly as effective as they think.

Customer retention does not come from sending out branded swag bags. Instead, it's injecting a personal and emotional experience into a sales relationship that inspires upselling, cross-selling, and revenue referral.

Why?

Suddenly that customer doesn't just view you in terms of product and price, but in terms of the value your company brings into their lives.

Our dear friend John Ruhlin runs a gift strategy and logistics company. An expert gifter, he advocates that you make the gift about the client, not your brand. And his company does just that, specializing in using gratitude to help companies cut through the noise, increase referrals, and create amazing customer experiences.

Ruhlin explains that it's not just the gift that counts; it's also the thoughtfulness behind it. With that in mind, he recommends giving gratitude when clients least expect it—shirking obvious dates like anniversaries, birthdays, and holidays—to surprise and delight them. He also thinks companies should go big, spending 10 percent of their annual revenue on showing their clients how grateful they are to have them. He says all this because, as we all know, loyalty is cheaper than acquisition.

When we facilitate vendor experiences on behalf of large companies, we find that both parties report more comradery, closeness, and celebration in what can otherwise be a very lonely space.

Of course, gratitude can make a big difference for employees too. When you take the time to get to know your people and build a culture of trust, where they can come into work and share what's going on in their world, people remember your kindness and honor it with the work they do.

In a recent study on how positive social emotions contribute to perseverance, David DeSteno, a professor of psychology at Northeastern University, found that feelings of pride, gratitude, and compassion increase tenacity by over 30 percent. And when we can make people feel grateful, they'll spend more time helping others, be more willing to take on leadership roles in groups, and work longer and harder to help their team solve a difficult problem. All the while, they'll feel more connected to the company, and stay longer. Wins all around.

## Gratitude Inquiry:

- *Reflection: What is one of the most meaningful gifts you have given to a client or partner?*


- *Reflection: What is one of the most meaningful gifts you have received from a vendor, supplier, or teammate?*


- *Action: Start planning your 2023 budget for allocating 10% of your revenue for gifting.*

# Send Customers Elsewhere

*"If we haven't got exactly what the customer wants we'll send him where he can get it. No high pressuring and forcing a customer to take something he doesn't really want. We'll be known as the helpful store, the friendly store, the store with a heart, the store that places public service ahead of profits. And, consequently, we'll make more profits than ever before."*
– Mr. Macy, *Miracle on 34th Street*

*Miracle on 34th Street* is a classic Christmas dramedy that takes place between Thanksgiving and Christmas Day in New York City.

In the movie, the real Santa Claus—a one Kris Kringle—is absolutely furious when he sees that the man assigned to play him in Macy's Thanksgiving Day Parade is drunk. When he tells the event's director, Doris Walker, about what he's observed, she urges him to fill the role himself. He's so convincing that he's hired to play Santa at Macy's on 34th Street in New York City.

This is when the true funny business begins. The head of the toy department, Julian Shellhammer, tells Kringle to direct undecided shoppers to the store's overstocked items. But when a woman approaches Kringle in search of a product Macy's didn't carry—a new bike—he suggests that she check out Gimbel's, Macy's competitor.

Kringle makes similar suggestions to other shoppers when Macy's doesn't have the gifts on their list. The store manager becomes so frustrated with his strategy that he suggests Santa undergo a psychological evaluation. I mean, who would steer paying customers to the store's competitors; the man MUST be crazy!

A few days later, Mr. Macy himself asks Kringle and Walker to come up to his office for a chat. When Kringle and Walker arrive, they see six men smoking cigars around Mr. Macy's big desk.

Mr. Macy says,

"I've been telling these gentlemen the new policy . . . you and Mr. Shellhammer initiated. I can't say that I approve of your not consulting the advertising department first but in the face of this tremendous public response I can't be angry with you. I admit this plan sounds idiotic and impossible. Imagine Macy's Santa Claus sending customers to Gimbels. Ho ho.

"But, gentlemen, you cannot argue with success. Look at this: telegrams, messages, telephone calls. The governor's wife, the mayor's wife, over thankful parents expressing undying gratitude to Macy's.

"Never in my entire career have I seen such a tremendous and immediate response to a merchandising policy. And I'm positive, Frank, if we expand our policy we'll expand our results as well.

"Therefore, from now on not only will our Santa Claus continue in this manner but I want every salesperson in this store to do precisely the same thing. If we haven't got exactly what the customer wants we'll send him where he can get it. No high pressuring and forcing a customer to take something he doesn't really want. We'll be known as the helpful store, the friendly store, the store with a heart, the store that places public service ahead of profits. And, consequently, we'll make more profits than ever before."

Kringle's genuine approach proved to be incredibly successful. People were so grateful for his honesty that they viewed the store in the same light—assuming that he was just carrying out a merchandising policy. As a result, they became diehard Macy's fans. And when it came time for their next purchase, you can bet Macy's was first on their list.

You can employ a similar strategy. If a client cancels business with you, don't forget to thank them. It might seem strange to thank someone for not doing business with you, or even choosing a competitor. But the best thing you can do is be empathetic to their situation and express gratitude for their interest or loyalty over the years.

When you give gratitude to a client, you strengthen that relationship. That will always be beneficial to you in the long run. The client who couldn't afford you this year, or who chose a competitor, could come back next year—and they may even pay a premium for your services. You never know, and it's always worth the effort.

# Gratitude Inquiry:

- *Reflection: When was the last time you refunded a client's payment or asked them to take their business elsewhere because you felt like you weren't the most qualified vendor for the objectives they wish to accomplish?*

- *Reflection: What network of partners are in your ecosystem that you can refer clients to at no charge, when they aren't a good fit for your business?*

- *Action: Reach out to a client or teammate who is no longer associated with your business and give them gratitude for all they meant to you while they were there.*

# Go Dark

*"Time well wasted is the best*
*kind of time spent."*
– Sean D'Souza

Companies are starting to make their own rules to support the well-being of those they serve. We saw this phenomenon firsthand while producing eight gratitude sessions for various teams at a publicly traded company in December 2020.

The sessions had been organized by the company's CTO and VPs of product. At the end of each session, the VPs came on screen to thank everyone for participating. Every time they joined, they told the team that they hoped everyone would leave with a different perspective, or some powerful realization that could carry them into the weekend and through the final days of the year. They also acknowledged what they had all been through over the past several months.

The leaders described what it had felt like for them to weather the challenges of COVID so far. They explained that the past several months had felt like an ultra marathon, during which they were in constant need of water. During the sessions, they acknowledged how much they appreciated the employees and the ways in which they had become leaders in their own right, and figured out ways to be creative and get things done with the utmost professionalism.

They acknowledged that the workplace fatigue they all felt was real, and that they wanted to make sure that there was an opportunity to step away for a moment and find rest and reflection, or to share the gratitude they felt. So, they were hosting a day of Digital Darkness.

The rest of that day was to be spent offline. That way, attendees could process some of what they had unearthed, or catch up on something that mattered to them. The leaders were walking their talk, showing their people how much they appreciated them by having them disconnect to reconnect with themselves.

In a world where being accessible at all times has become the norm, that meant something. And it meant that when employees logged back on, they felt more loyal, connected, and grateful to be there.

## Gratitude Inquiry:

- *Reflection: If you were given 6 hours off work for the rest of your day, right now, what would you do? How would you recharge? What would that time mean to you?*

- *Reflection: What new insights do you hope your team would gather if you gave them an entire day off, free of technology? How would the energy or perspective of the team shift?*


- *Action: Schedule a 6- hour block on your team's calendar starting at 11:00 am. Once they show up, surprise them by giving them the balance of the day off for a Digital Detox.*

# Use Gratitude to Reenergize Sales—and Everything Else

*"There are no limits to the good you can bring forth to you, and by practicing gratitude daily, you will increase and maximize your magnetic power to attract a life beyond your wildest dreams."*
– Rhonda Byrne

One of our clients experienced a similar challenge to many other businesses during the COVID-19 pandemic: their sales numbers were low, along with team morale.

There were many factors contributing to their problems. A large portion of the team had just been hired and hadn't had the opportunity to meet their coworkers in person. Rather than enjoying the high-energy, collaborative in-office culture that had been in place before the pandemic began, new hires were working from home. As a result, they were uncomfortable with each other; it just didn't feel like a cohesive team environment. And though they had worked hard, due to conditions outside their control, they hadn't achieved their quotas. Their sales division had struggled all quarter and needed a creative way to get inspired for the final quarter of the year.

The company's leadership was worried, and not just about the numbers: they realized the potential for resignations was at an all-time high. So, they reached out to 7:47 to produce a custom team-building experience that would help generate positive energy and increase engagement among the group.

By partnering with 7:47, our clients hoped to make their remote work environment feel more inclusive, exciting, and inviting for both new and tenured employees. They hoped that our Virtual Gratitude Experience™ would make their salespeople feel more appreciative of their jobs *and* more connected to their peers. Ideally, their staff would develop a greater sense of belonging and a stronger sense of purpose—to feel as if they were a part of something bigger than themselves.

From a sales standpoint, they wanted their team to learn the techniques necessary to empathize with their customer base— how to listen actively, how to create safe space, how to ask deep follow-up questions, and how to respond to the feelings and perspectives of those they served. They anticipated that, by increasing their daily motivation, inspiring them with positivity, and offering new tools and resources for collaboration, their team would create deeper connections with their customers and drive new revenue.

Our Virtual Gratitude Experience™ acted as the kickoff event for a month-long gratitude-centric sales campaign. The goal that month was for each Account Executive to make at least 100 calls to express their gratitude and appreciation for their customers. Whether these were existing customers, prospects, or even canceled accounts, the primary focus was building genuine connections and generating positive momentum for their other sales efforts.

Before going through our experience and starting their calls, we surveyed each employee to get a firm understanding of how they felt emotionally. That provided us with a means of determining what type of impact or change our program could make on their team over the course of the thirty-day process.

Twenty-one out of thirty participants (a whopping 70 percent) provided either negative or very negative feedback on the survey. They described themselves as feeling "tired," "nervous," "cautious," "anxious," and "overwhelmed." Others felt "fatigued," "burnt out," and "scattered."

With those answers, we knew we had our work cut out for us. But we made tremendous progress in a short period of time. The experience helped them come together and gain a better understanding of how to function as salespeople in the challenging remote environment that the pandemic had birthed.

Our client's team underwent an undeniably positive emotional transformation while working with our team. During the last few sessions, the negative sentiments employees had shared at the beginning of the month were replaced with words like "thankful," "nostalgic," "connected," "reflective," and "grateful." Overall, each participant felt better about their work, team, and employer by the time we finished working together.

By the end of the thirty-day Virtual Gratitude Experience™, all thirty team members felt positive or very positive about their work environment. Participants reported feelings of gratitude, connectedness, happiness, and joy upon exiting the program. Many of them had what they considered life-changing experiences that affected both their professional and personal lives during the conversations we facilitated, and some of them wrote in after our breakout groups asking to be connected to those they had spoken with to keep the conversations alive.

Because our program was such a success, our client expressed interest in connecting us to other teams within their company to produce similarly effective experiences for them.

They hope their account executives and other customer-facing employees can take what they've learned through working with us and apply it toward making deeper, meaningful connections with their peers and customers alike.

But it's not just about one-off events, or even a series of Gratitude Experiences. To continue feeling the effects of gratitude, you must incorporate it in ritual form, engaging with it regularly.

## Gratitude Inquiry:

- *Reflection: After reading Section 5, how are you currently feeling about work and your work responsibilities? Be honest!*

- *Reflection: If your clients had to describe in one word how they feel right now, what would they say and what are you doing to show them greater empathy?*

- *Action: Commit to spending the next 30 days by sending video messages, gifts, or other forms of gratitude to at least 100 of your clients or customers.*

# PART VI

# Build Rituals to Make It Through

*"Gratitude is a currency that we can mint*
*for ourselves, and spend without fear of bankruptcy."*
-Fred De Witt Van Amburgh

# Develop Your Gratitude Rituals— and Do Them Pro-socially

*"It's impossible to be grateful and unhappy. If you want to be happy, you have to be grateful. But the practice of feeling grateful is working a muscle. It's not an emotion. It's an exercise that you must complete on a frequent basis."*
– Shannon Eusey

I checked into my first rehab program on May 14, 2008.

I barely recognize the person I was before that date. I spent money with abandon, fraternized with a dangerous crowd, and even crashed a few cars. I didn't feel good about the life I was living, but I didn't know how to change.

The day before I was scheduled to start rehab, I went on a bender. I hopped on the plane drunk and I landed at a Utah airport hungover, where two goons picked me up to escort me to a local motel. They guarded my motel room the entire night, and stayed with me until I checked into the program the following morning.

The program was originally founded under the name Wilderness Conquest, with the goal of helping convicts reintegrate into society. Similar to the intake process in jail, where I'd been a few times before then, they stripped me down to my skivvies and confiscated all my material possessions.

Then, they gave me:

- Three pairs of underwear
- Three pairs of socks
- One pair of boots
- Two pairs of pants
- One moisture-wicking shirt
- Two jackets
- One sleeping bag
- An 8' x 10' military tarp
- Ninety feet of military parachute cord
- Two army surplus backpack straps
- One lunch bag
- A notepad
- The Big Book of Alcoholics Anonymous
- A workbook
- A few pencils

"All right, off you go," the guards said. Then, they loaded me into a car alongside all my new gear, and we drove close to one hundred miles into the Manti-La Sal National Forest, where I joined the other people who were already in the program. Our sole objective was to use topographical maps to get from point A to point B to point C to point D—and to survive.

Oh, and spill our guts to the counselors along the way.

We received food drops on Tuesdays and Saturdays, which meant new seasoning packets, dry rice and beans, brown sugar,

SPAM®, and—what quickly became my favorite item—peanut butter.

At the time, peanut butter was all I had to look forward to in life. I'd scoop a spoonful from the jar and top it with brown sugar, savoring every bite. I even carved a spoon out of a Ponderosa pine branch, and tucked a serving into my cheek just before I fell asleep. That it only came on Saturdays made it even more of a treat.

There I was, in the most pivotal two months of my life, and all I cared about was peanut butter. Yes, I'd made a good habit of sitting by the campfire at night with Mitch and dreaming about what life on the outside would look like. But those were just dreams. Peanut butter was real. I could taste it, sleep with it, sniff it, and savor it. All I had to do was appreciate it and go slow so that it would last until the next ration.

Pretty soon, I started developing gratitude for this peanut butter. With all the turmoil happening in my life, I was grateful for the true simplicity of this newfound ritual. It's what got me through those arduous first two (of many) months in rehab. It gave me a sense of hope and optimism—even pride and self-confidence in that I could set the small goal of making it last and celebrate peanut butter's arrival every Saturday. It made me believe that I could tackle bigger goals too.

More importantly, it didn't happen in a vacuum. There was a whole group of other people there with whom I could reflect on all I'd been through, everything my experiences had taught me, and the many benefits that lay ahead if I could get my shit together. I talked to them about the big stuff, and about the peanut butter too.

Thankfully, you don't need to go to rehab to learn to appreciate the power of gratitude rituals. You may be more familiar with the process than you think.

You may have grown up with religious rituals that connect you to your faith, or cultural rituals passed down from ancestors that connect you to your heritage. Hell, even rituals around dressing up in your favorite team's gear and going to the game.

Those experiences can create a deep affinity between the people who share them. But too often they are too few and far apart—events to which we count down on the calendar and not an integral part of our daily lives.

Instead, the daily rituals we tend to adopt revolve around fueling up with caffeine and winding down with alcohol. And instead of enjoying those rituals with others, we grab coffee from the drive-through and finish a bottle of wine over the latest bingeable show on Netflix.

But building those rituals pro-socially is worth the effort. It doesn't just connect you to the people who share your identity; it cultivates deep and meaningful relationships with people who come from all walks of life. And we can start just as small as I did with my peanut butter—that's what rituals are all about.

Take a friend or colleague with you on your daily coffee run. Tell them why you're glad they're in your life. Do it early and often.

We can all connect through a desire to show and share gratitude. Our lives will be better for it. And the more we do it, the better they'll be.

## Gratitude Inquiry:

- *Reflection: Similar to my experience with peanut butter, has there been a turning point in your life when a ritual helped you through something difficult?*


- *Reflection: What is one ritual of solitude you have in your life right now? What would it look like to share that ritual with others?*


- *Action: Make a list of the daily rituals at work or in your personal life that you've not given enough credit or thanks to. Give gratitude to the simplicity of their nature.*

# Send Video Tributes



We can use gratitude to help others going through a tough time. And though displays of gratitude are particularly meaningful to the recipient when they are inconvenient for the giver, sometimes we need more efficient options. My friend Andrew Horn has been offering one for years through his company, Tribute.

It all began when Andrew's wife, Miki, sent an email to twenty of Andrew's closest friends and family members and asked them to send in a video telling Andrew why they loved him or how he had made an impact on their lives. The result of her request was a twenty-minute video montage that was the most meaningful gift Andrew had ever received.

After hearing how difficult it was for Miki to create the tribute, Andrew had a lightbulb moment. Tribute was born. What started as a simple gift, grew into a business and movement to help the masses experience the same joy that Andrew felt when he received the video.

Tribute's software makes it easy to collect and share messages of love and appreciation. Gather the email addresses of friends and family, import them into Tribute, and the software does the rest, sending emails to everyone requesting video tributes, collecting their submissions, and editing them into a beautiful short film. Over 82 percent of recipients cry tears of joy when they receive their video. The Tribute team is truly on a mission to spread gratitude and build human connection.

I received a tribute for my 30th birthday from my girlfriend, Molly.She had taken the time to collect email addresses of my loved ones, input them into the program, and click send on the campaign.From there, Tribute sent requests and then followed up with all my friends to create a video for me.They sent the montage via youtube and I cried within the first thirty seconds.

Since their inception, over five million gratitude videos have been shared through the platform, making Tribute #269 on 2021's Inc. 500—among the top 10 percent of Inc. 5000's fastest-growing privately held businesses in the country! The company's meteoric growth is testament to just how much people are craving gratitude in these tough times. It also provides meaningful insight into when and how people want to give and receive gratitude.

While your first instinct might be to express your gratitude in such a way when someone in your life experiences a happy milestone, like a birthday or anniversary, doing it when they're down in the dumps will likely have an even greater impact.

Just as giving gratitude can lift us up when we're struggling, receiving gratitude can make a major difference in the lives of our colleagues, friends, and family when times are tough. So, when someone you care about is hurting, hit record and watch the magic happen—for both of you.

# Gratitude Inquiry:

- *Reflection: Have you ever received a video tribute? How did it feel to receive credit both verbally and visually? Rewind and watch it today.*

- *Reflection: If you had to send a barrage of gratitude to someone right now, who needed it more than anything else in the world, what does that look like? What community of people would you like to participate or get involved?*

- *Action: Sign up for Tribute.com and start a campaign for the person you mentioned above!*

# Embark on a Gratitude Walk-and-Talk

*"Walking the grounds of gratitude*
*I stumbled upon the palace of happiness."*
– Brendon Burchard

Giving gratitude is a pretty intimate experience. When you tell someone why they matter to you, you're automatically vulnerable. With that in mind, while sharing gratitude face-to-face is powerful, sometimes the prospect is too overwhelming—particularly in a work environment.

Gratitude walk-and-talks can help you reap all the benefits of a gratitude ritual while avoiding some of the awkwardness.

Pair people up for a daily gratitude walk-and-talk session, and send them out into the wild. The goal of each walk should be to share gratitude while observing your surroundings. And while trekking the halls of your building will work, if you take it outside, you'll deepen the positive impact even further by combining all that gratitude has to offer with the benefits of spending time in nature.

When you connect outdoors, taking in the smell of the trees, the sounds of the birds, and the colors and textures outside the four walls of your office, you are investing in your well-being and that of your team. Studies show that as few as five minutes of so-called "green exercise" can boost your mood and increase self-esteem. All of these activities are linked to a reduction in symptoms associated with depression, stress, and anxiety.

When you combine the benefits of gratitude with those of waking in nature, they compound. Braiding together the science-backed benefits of sharing gratitude, getting exercise, and spending time outdoors, you extend the effectiveness of gratitude. I'd say that's worth building a ritual around.

## Gratitude Inquiry:

- *Reflection: What parts of nature speak to you most? Is it the sound of the chirping birds, running water, the smell of the trees,or the colors of the botanicals?*

- *Reflection:Where is your go-to spot to escape from the world?*

- *Action: Make a plan to visit a special spot in nature this week for a gratitude walk-and-talk. Who would you like to invite to join you??Practice peer-to-peer gratitude on that walk.*

# Celebrate Small Wins



Have you ever struggled to accomplish a big goal?

In traditional goal-setting, you haven't accomplished anything until you hit your goal. For 99.99% of the time, until you *finally* hit that target, you're failing. That can be disheartening enough to keep you from achieving what you set out to do. And the harder the starting conditions, the more daunting that goal feels.

To succeed, you have to break down that goal into more manageable pieces, creating a journey with checkpoints to be celebrated along the way.

Mark your progress with quick bursts of gratitude, especially in a team environment. Thank the people with whom you are collaborating for helping you make it that far. Sharing peer-to-peer gratitude when working together to accomplish micro-goals that add up to big ones—that creates momentum.

Our friends Seth Bader and Luis Scott host a fifteen-minute, all-hands meeting every Monday morning at work. They call them huddles. The theme is usually gratitude, and they spend the time elevating each other. Our friend Shane Metcalf at 15Five actually invented a gratitude platform to recognize, appreciate, and celebrate small wins. It's available to both the internal team and to clients, so that everyone can share the wealth of gratitude. Through the platform, his team gives each other about 700 high fives each week, and clients share at least one million high fives each month. These small acts ultimately make a major difference in what they accomplish.

A recent study supports the connection between goal attainment and gratitude. Participants were told to make a shortlist of goals they wanted to accomplish over a period of two months, and then broken into two groups and instructed to start journaling about their progress. One group was instructed to keep a journal focused on gratitude, while the other was told to journal more generally.

At the end of the period, participants were asked to share their progress toward their end goal. Those who were in the gratitude journaling condition felt that they made more progress than those who weren't.

So, break it up, and give thanks for the people who helped you make it each step of the way. It will bring you closer to each other—and closer to the finish line.

## Gratitude Inquiry:

- *Reflection: In the past, did you find it difficult to celebrate the small wins in your life? What is the reason?*

- *Reflection: Name one small, almost insignificant win you've had recently? Who is that one person that helped you achieve it?*

277

- *Action: Choose three people in your sphere to give a metaphorical "high five" to this week for something small they've accomplished.*

# Write It Out

*"If the only prayer you ever say in your
entire life is thank you, it will be enough."*
– Meister Eckhart

My friend Gina Hamadey engaged in a powerful gratitude exercise, one that lasted a whole year. She wrote at least one thank-you note every day, more than 365 thank-you notes in total—addressing them to family members, friends, neighbors, and even strangers—and documented the process in a book called *I Want to Thank You: How a Year of Gratitude Can Bring Joy and Meaning in a Disconnected World.*

When I learned about her project, my mind immediately jumped to the potential awkwardness of some of those exchanges. It even addressed some of the anxieties I had about giving gratitude.

*What if someone didn't acknowledge her note?*

*What if they were confused as to why she was thanking them?*

*What if they didn't even remember the act to which she was referring?*

I asked Gina how she got past those concerns. For her, letting go of any expectation or anxiety about hearing back from the recipients was key. Gina told herself that it didn't matter whether they got back to her. The goal was not to invoke reciprocity; it was to make her gratitude known. That was a reward in and of itself.

During his time as Campbell's CEO, Douglas Conant sent more than 30,000 handwritten thank-you notes to his employees. He found his letters improved morale and productivity, while keeping him connected to his team. They would often write back, including stories that provided valuable insight about what they were going through. By paying attention—and listening—carefully, he built trust and earned their engagement.

A side effect of the culture of gratitude Conant created? Improved performance. When Conant took charge of Campbell Soup in 2001, it was the worst-performing major food company in the world. By 2009, it ranked among the Best Global Brands (and drew additional accolades for its excellent culture and corporate citizenship).

Research attests to the mood-boosting effects of such efforts. Kent State University professor Steve Toepfer dug into the psychological benefits of gratitude letters with his 2009 study. Students who wrote regular gratitude letters reported more life satisfaction and happiness and less depression than those who didn't.

Ready to embark on your own gratitude letter-writing ritual? Here are some tips to make each missive count:

- Make it as personal as possible. Picture the person you're thanking right in the room with you, and write the way you'd speak to them: from the heart
- Be specific about why you're grateful for them. Tell the story of when, where, and how they made an impact on you

- Tell them how you'll be paying their kindness forward, if possible
- It's about progress, not perfection. Don't worry about your penmanship. Sloppy handwriting and poor grammar is fine! The message will come through loud and clear, regardless of how neat it looks

I now keep a set of letters and stamps right next to my desk, in case the urge to write out my gratitude arises. I've even grown to love a wonderful artist named Jillian Kaye that draws out beautiful paintings on letterhead as part of the gratitude process!

## Gratitude Inquiry:

- *Reflection: Have you experienced the feeling of expressing gratitude to someone and it wasn't recognized? What thoughts were going through your mind?*

- *Reflection: Have you ever made the decision to refrain from writing a gratitude letter because you assumed potential awkwardness?*

- *Action: It's time to get in the habit of establishing a gratitude letter-writing ritual. Make a list of 10 people you can send a letter to. What fun elements can you incorporate to put your unique mark on these letters (ex: using a fancy pen to write them, choosing stationary from an artist you love, or including a poem)?*

# Soak It In

*"It is our duty to bestow benefits upon ourselves,
therefore we ought to be grateful to ourselves."*
– Seneca

By now you know that giving gratitude is invaluable, but don't forget yourself in the process.

During times of trouble, many people view their personal prospects from a perspective of scarcity. They convince themselves that they'll never get through these troubling times.

Why?

They imagine they just don't have enough resources. They convince themselves they have a small network, small opportunities, a small bank account. But you can turn that scarcity mindset into one of sufficiency.

In her book *The Soul of Money: Transforming Your Relationship with Money and Life*, Lynne Twist describes a conversation she had with a woman named Audrey. Audrey got married young, and that relationship ended unhappily. Her husband divorced her and took all her money. She was left with nothing—at least financially.

She and Twist met during the dark period that followed the divorce. After Audrey shared what happened, Twist challenged her to write down the names of twenty people who had given her a compliment or appreciated something about her (at 7:47, we would classify those as "benefits").

Next, Twist asked Audrey to make a list of the adjectives they would use to describe her—words like clever, courageous, brave, beautiful, bold, funny, witty, sincere.

Twist then helped her realize that these qualities she had—ones most people take an entire lifetime to develop—couldn't be bought. Moreover, Audrey was already being recognized for them.

With that insight, Audrey's life changed. She no longer determined her self-worth by the money she had. She became optimistic, knowing that there were still amazing people in her life that valued her tremendously. She would be able to get out of these dark times, relying on the attributes she already possessed.

She would go on to design and create a vision for her future, without the baggage of her husband. Then, she would then bring those twenty people together, introduce them to one another, give them gratitude, and create so much well-being and life-affirming feelings across the group.

Sometimes getting through tough times starts with recognizing our worth, and the benefit we provide others just by existing. More than money, material possessions, and even acts of kindness, our worth resides in our inherent qualities, and it's worth taking the time to recognize that.

Lists like the one Audrey made can help. But you can't just set it and forget it; you've got to remind yourself of how much you have to be grateful for on a regular basis. Make that list, then make a ritual of returning to it to expand on it.

# Gratitude Inquiry:

- *Reflection: What are the negative stories you go over in your mind during troubling times? For example: my network is too small, I have no opportunities, the resources aren't there.*

- *Reflection: Who are some people in your community who entered your life during a period of challenge or transition? How is your relationship with them different from other connections you have?*

- *Action: Ask five people closest to you to provide you feedback on three values they appreciate and admire about you and a few stories about how you have impacted their lives.Take note of similar themes in the values reflected back to you.*

# Forgive Yourself

*"I think that forgiveness should be one of your core values. We often extoll the importance of forgiving others that have wronged us. But how often do we forgive ourselves? That is often the harder thing to do."*
– Chester Elton

The Monday after my non-suicidal self-injury episode, I had a call with one of my teammates.

I explained what had happened the previous week, and I told her how sorry I was. I had put my own life in jeopardy, but in the process, I'd also jeopardized her livelihood.

In the wake of what I'd done, all I felt was shame and guilt and anger, and I'd spent the past four days apologizing to everyone around me.

I apologized to Molly, because she had been there in person. I apologized to my mom, because she'd been on the phone. I apologized to my dad, in case he was embarrassed to have raised a son who wasn't perfect. I apologized to my friends for requiring so much support.

Now, on the call, I was explaining how sorry I was once again. I told her that I knew my actions could have had an impact on her finances, her career trajectory, her ability to find joy, and even her ability to have a positive impact on others.

"You don't have to apologize to me," she said. "Have you apologized to yourself? Have you forgiven yourself for what happened?"

I hadn't.

Just then, I realized that was the work I had left to do and that it would likely be the hardest work of all.

Why?

True healing starts with self-forgiveness. When I could forgive myself, I could stop apologizing and start giving gratitude, thanking the people in my life for all they had done to show up for me.

As soon as the call ended, I messaged my friend and one of the world's best healers, Grace Smith. "I need you, desperately," I wrote. Through a series of hypnotherapy sessions, she and Brooke from her team helped me appreciate my own inner strengths. With their support, I began the process of self-forgiveness. It started with a ritual.

Take a nice, deep, letting go breath and repeat:

*I feel relief. I am satisfied. I appreciate all I have.*
*I feel relief. I am satisfied. I appreciate all I have.*
*I feel relief. I am satisfied. I appreciate all I have.*

Take the time to truly feel the relief a moment of gratitude can grant you . . .

Now, amplify and magnify that feeling of gratitude.

Amplify and magnify that feeling of gratitude.

Amplify and magnify that feeling of gratitude.

Enjoy your mental freedom and have a wonderful day!

Our sessions were hours-long moments of bliss and transformation for me. Brooke and Grace helped me reconnect with my inner child and find self-compassion. The experience was extraordinary.

Another friend had a suggestion as to how I could activate self-love and self-compassion.

"To feel self-compassion at a cellular level," she said, "I would sit and cry in the mirror, using the brain's mirror neurons to kickstart chemicals for empathy. We are hard wired to respond to one another's pain, and when you see another human (who just happens to be you!) in pain, it's extremely hard not to feel compassion.

"You start to soften, and then for me, the floodgates of compassion and—eventually, over time—self-love opened. I hope it helps you in the same way it helped me."

She was explaining that we can cultivate empathy for ourselves when we take the time to see the pain we're in, and consider it the way we would consider a friend's pain. And then we can give gratitude to that empathetic person for holding space for us.

With both these rituals on board, I'm on the path to self-forgiveness, self-compassion, and a whole lot more gratitude.

## Gratitude Inquiry:

- *Reflection: What does the word "self-forgiveness" mean to you?*

- *Reflection: What are some situations in your past that would benefit from practicing self-forgiveness? Would you feel a sense of relief?*


- *Action: Create a self-forgiveness ritual for yourself, one that would take 15 minutes or less. Try to commit each week. Visit getgrace.com for examples of self-forgiveness rituals*

# Cultivate Self-Compassion

*"We did not feel prepared to be the heirs of such a terrifying hour. But within it we found the power to author a new chapter, to offer hope and laughter to ourselves."*
– Amanda Gorman

Sometimes finding self-compassion starts with letting others into your life.

In June of 2019, I had the great opportunity to interview Simon Berg, CEO of Ceros, a digital design platform. Just a month or so later, I made him an offer. I asked if I could come to his home in New Jersey, and cook dinner for him and eighteen of his closest friends. Simon agreed to have me over, and we set a date: Wednesday, August 7.

On Monday, August 5, just two days before the dinner, my phone rang. It was Simon. "Chris," he said, "I have been in somewhat of a funk in my life recently. Just today, I pictured what it would look like if I wasn't here. I didn't like what I saw, so I've moved on from that thought."

"But I'm not really in the mood to be social. If I had made plans with anyone else this week, I'd have canceled them. But because it's you, and because I have an inkling of what you have planned, I think it might change my life."

On Wednesday, I climbed into an Uber with two folding tables, enough chairs for the group, and bags and bags of cooking equipment. When my ride got stuck in the Holland Tunnel, Simon came to get me.

In his car, he elaborated on what he had shared earlier. "My company's growing at an incredible rate. I have an incredible family. I feel like I have everything I could ever want. But I just don't appreciate any of it. I don't have any self-compassion."

I told him I wished I could help him, but I struggled with the same issue. I felt as if my own self-compassion was nowhere to be found.

We set up the tables and I moved to the kitchen, falling into a rhythm that had become familiar over the past few years.

Soon, the guests arrived and we all sat down to dinner. The minute the group began sharing, Simon started to cry. The tears didn't stop for three straight hours. He was soaked in love, connection, and the compassion his community showed him. And in that moment, he finally began to find compassion for himself. It changed everything.

He and I both began working with Grace Smith, the healer who has helped me time and again. His company launched new products, raised more money, and reached new heights. And most importantly, he came to appreciate what he had and the work he had done to bring it to life.

Around the same time, I met another person who would become a crucial figure in helping *me* find self-compassion. I interviewed a man named Ben Wright on my podcast. He was the founder of the fourth-fastest growing company in the country. Everything was taking off for Ben.

When I found out that I would be speaking at a conference in Denver—his hometown—that September, I asked if I could come cook him dinner. I offered him the same set-up that I had put together for Simon: I'd bring over two six-foot tables and cook dinner for him and eighteen of his closest friends.

He accepted, and we had a wonderful night of human connection. Everyone cried once again, Ben shared his gratitude with all of us, and a brotherhood was born.

Every time I felt like an imposter or a monster—at any hour of the day—I'd call Ben, and we'd talk through our anxieties. I was, and always will be, honored to have him in my corner. Ben is a family man who builds great companies, serves his community, gives gratitude where gratitude is due, and shows up for the people in his life. And by showing up for me, he helped me show myself compassion.

Whenever I need a reminder to be kinder to myself, I turn to Ben and Simon. And I try to pay forward all that they've provided me.

If you're struggling to cultivate self-compassion, think about the people in your community who can remind you of your value. Then, turn around and do the same for others, sharing the benefits they have offered you. The result is a legacy of gratitude that continues to pay dividends to everyone it touches.

# Gratitude Inquiry:

- *Reflection: Name the persons you let into your life at a deeper level?*

- *Reflection: Are there parts of your life where you "should" feel happy or accomplished, but you haven't reached that point? How could you cultivate self-compassion for yourself in these areas?*

- *Action: Have an honest conversation with someone in your community (refer to the list from the "soak it up" section) who can remind you of your value this week. Share what you're going through and ask for their support in cultivating self-compassion!*

# Leave a Legacy of Gratitude

*"Let us prepare our minds as if we'd come to the very end of life. Let us postpone nothing. Let us balance life's books each day. . . . The one who puts the finishing touches on their life each day is never short of time."*
– Seneca

I already told you a bit about my friend Sandy Gibson. He is co-founder and CIO of Better Place Forests, a natural alternative for cemeteries. The company offers memorial trees as resting places for cremated remains in protected forests. That means he thinks a lot about life, death, and one's legacy. "Planning for the end of your life is almost like pre-gratitude—like it's going to happen, it's going to hurt. How do you make something beautiful out of it?" he said.

He went on to tell me a story about his dad. "I love going to baseball games because my dad was just the same. He didn't really watch sports too much. He watched a little bit on TV, but he loved going to baseball games. I came to love them too. Every time I go to a baseball game, I think about the connection I had with my father. And I think if we're intentional about it, we can help show other folks who care about us and who we care about, how to have that connection with us even after we're gone."

What do we owe our ancestors for their sacrifice? Sacrifice of ourselves, for the betterment of others. What if we aimed to improve the lives of those around us, based on what we learned from someone we loved? What if we made gratitude part of their legacy—and our own?

You can't pay it back. You have to pay it forward. You have to keep that legacy alive. And you can start with simple acts that honor the people who gave you a benefit, every single day.

I've spent this entire book attempting to help you understand the benefits you've received from others. But you've got to realize the benefits others receive from you—and the ones you'll continue to provide down the line, and even after you're gone.

It's very easy for us to overlook the impact we've had on others. Diving into that impact, and keeping it front and center is one way to be of great service and support to others going forward, in meaningful ways.

So, do it for the people in your life who did so much for you—living or dead. Do it for your own well-being, or the well-being of those you love, or the well-being of a stranger who could really use your support and reassurance. Do it to make the world a little less harsh, even during the hardest of times. But don't forget to recognize your own impact, make it count, and give gratitude for that.

When you do, the world will thank you in ways big and small, and if you open yourself up to that gratitude, it will change your life—and your legacy.

# Gratitude Inquiry:

- *Reflection: What legacies are present in your daily life as a result of family members and teachers who have passed away? What benefits did you derive from their legacy?*

- *Reflection: What are you currently devoting your time, energy, and resources on that could contribute to the legacy you wish to leave?*

- *Action: Give yourself the gift of 30 minutes each week writing about your legacy and watch how it shifts the actions you take on a daily basis. Years from now, when you are no longer around, how do you want to be remembered, and what do you want people to say about you?*

# Acknowledgments

As our friend, Mark Messier, says in his book, *No One Wins Alone*, "this book is itself an example of the amazing people who have supported me throughout my life. It *is* the acknowledgement."

Writing this book has been an incredible and rewarding experience and could not have been possible without the collaboration of a wonderful team. I'm so grateful for the continued support and love of my best friend and partner, Molly Sovran, my parents, Phil and Carol Schembra, and Lynn Goins. Together, the five of us survived a pandemic together as a core unit, with some more severe than others, but we persevered nonetheless.

Dr. Debi and Mike Lynes - You see me.Thank you for always lending a non-judgemental ear and for lighting a fire in my brain to complete this book. Amigo's and Liquid Deaths in your kitchen are the moments we live for.

My heartfelt gratitude to our amazing team at 7:47. You showed up for people during their darkest hour, and put in meaningful work to inspire and motivate them. Thank you to Jennifer Cunningham and Sonia Corredor, our two longest tenured teammates for sticking with us through the hardest of times. Our year began as we welcomed Jasmine Bennett, Madeline Haslam, and David Nebrinski to the team.What a wild journey it has been.

To our closest childhood friends, mentors, family, members of Club Armada, HHP Class of '06, lifelong friends and fraternity brothers from Rollins, Rock the Vibe, and Da Boyz crew, thank you for all your inspiration and friendship.

A special pandemic shoutout to our closest and dear New York City friends for the comfort you've provided - Scott Marchfeld and Kaitlyn Hogan, Alec and Shauna Hajdukovich, Sean and Leslie Clifford, Chris and Paige Sanborn, Stephen Sokoler and Ita Koren, Bill and Lauren Tyndall, Steve and Lilly Tam, Andy and Maddie Ellwood, Jonathan and Cas Palmer, Tripp Derrick Barnes, Nile Lundgren, Kris and Kathleen Gross, Josiah Ryan, Paul and Lauren Vecchione, Nathan and Flavia Aycock, and Dave Lindsey.

Sara Stibitz and Brianne Sanchez - Your contributions and encouragement helped birth the beginning of this book.You sat on my zoom calls with Madeline and me for months as I worked through the unknown craziness of what my vision was for this book.

Ariel Hubbard and Marley Pine - You closed out this book in amazing fashion. You've completed every one of the sentences we started, and the collaboration has been seamless.Thank you for lending your editorial and writing skills to this body of work.

Charlie Fusco and John Michael Esposito - Over lunch, producing conferences, and giggling across time zones, we've dreamed up mischief and made it happen. Thank you for entrusting me with so many opportunities with your crew. I am proud to share you with mine.

The Arcbound Team - You have amplified our voice over the past year and a half, broadcasting the principles of gratitude to so many.

Tyler Wagner - Dang my man, Miami is on fire with you down there. Thank you for putting your marketing machine behind this book.

Tiffani Bova - Although we have only known each other for two years, it seems like a lifetime. Beginning with Dorie's virtual experience, to keynoting Salesforce, to Tiffani Bova dinners, and so much more. Your knowledge is endless, your passion for teaching is inspiring.

Chester Elton - For your late night phone calls. Experimental clubhouse rooms. Conversations about gratitude, and so much more. You paved the way for so many of us. You forged paths our industry never knew existed. When will you slow down? I hope no time soon.

Scott Gerber and Ryan Paugh - My heartfelt thanks for your invitation to write for your publications, Rolling Stone and Fast Company. It's incredible and insane how you have a dream or vision and then build epic communities around it.

Brenda Hudson - Meeting and working beside you, serving your team, and signing your book was actually a pivotal moment that probably saved my life. I was signing your book while being robbed in my own home, and our conversations in Austin gave me a new breath of fresh air. Your confidence in me during this writing process has been legendary. I can't wait to follow you on your next journey, I'll always be in your corner.

Lori Cornmesser and Cedric Griffin -I was deeply honored to join you in Napa for Lori's 50th birthday party and didn't give it a second thought that I wanted to attend. The two of you have always seen me, just as I see you. It's been such a thrilling ride to build out our Belonging Series with the two of you.

Daniel, Marc, and Asha Masci - To infinity and beyond! Co-founding 7:47 Gratitude Australia, our first international joint venture has been an incredible learning opportunity. You have a proven track record of building, and I'm honored that the principles of gratitude are your next venture.

David Goldstein - Maestro of experiences extraordinaire. Congratulations on building one of the world's fastest growing companies by helping people connect and find their place in our society. Your leadership has given me permission to dive head first into our craft. You've busted down doors so that providers like us can step in and serve.

Lynn Turkington and Scuderia Ferrari - Class, dignity, integrity, history, community. Lynn, time is our greatest asset, and you've given Molly and me an amazing experience to have the opportunity to spend so much time together in support of. The world is so fortunate to have you and the team in it. Forza Ferrari!

Lisa Penn - At 4:30 PM on December 30th, 2021, you looked across my zoom and noticed an unmistakable weariness. Your intuition suggested we end the meeting early, and for me to take a rest. That night, I would engage in the largest act of non suicidal self injury of my life. Your intuition is what guides you, and your love for others is bold and infectious. Thank you for letting me see you. And thank you in return for seeing me.

Court Roberts and Lilly Callahan - The two of you helped us codify and build upon our experiences. You've opened up new pathways in the way we look at our programs, and thus more impact can be had.

To those of you who have invited us into your home, knowing that my greatest insecurity is being the last one called to the party. Thank you.

To those of you who have answered my calls at midnight or during a big depressive mood and talked with me until the wee hours of the morning. Thank you.

To those of you who have come into our home, bringing a bottle of wine, and engaging in vulnerable conversations around the campfire. Thank you.

To those of you who showed up to those early Virtual Gratitude Experiences for our community, and supported each other during your greatest times of need. Thank you.

To those of our clients and close partners who have invited us during the past few years to produce Virtual Gratitude Experiences for your teams. Thank you.

To those of you who called, texted, cooked for me, and sent emails after my non-suicidal self injury. Thank you.

To those of you who said yes to becoming a guest on my podcast, and allowing me to ask you my unscripted, radical questions. Thank you.

To those of you that allowed us to quote them for this book. Thank you.

# References

## Introduction


Seneca, Translated by Miriam Griffin and Brad Inwood. *On Benefits.* University of Chicago Press, 2011.

Taleb, Nassim N. *Antifragile: Things That Gain From Disorder.* Random House, 2012, p. 156.

Holiday, Ryan. *The Obstacle is the Way: The Timeless Art of Turning Trials into Triumph.* Penguin, 2014.

Emmons, R. A. and Joanna Hill. *Words of gratitude: For Mind, Body, and Soul.* Templeton Foundation Press, 2001.

David Hume. *A Treatise of Human Nature.* Book 3, Part 1, Section 1. "Moral Distinctions not Derived from Reason." Edited by L.A. Selby-Bigge. Oxford: Clarendon Press, 1888.

Kant, Immanuel. *Lectures on Ethics.* Translated by Louis Infield, Hackett, 1980.

de Waal, Frans. *The Age of Empathy.* Crown, 2010.

Joiner, Thomas E. *Lonely at the Top.* Palgrave Macmillan, 2011.

Murthy, Vivek H. *Together: The Healing Power of Human Connection in a Sometimes Lonely World.* Harper Collins, 2020.

Killam, Kasley. "To Combat Loneliness, Promote Social Health." *Scientific American*, Springer Nature, 23 Jan. 2018, www.scientificamerican.com/article/to-combat-loneliness -promote-social-health1/.

Waldinger, Robert. "What Makes a Good Life? Lessons From the Longest Study on Happiness." *TEDxBeaconStreet*, 14 Nov. 2015, www.ted.com/talks/robert_waldinger_what_makes_a_good_life_lessons_from_the_longest_study_on_happiness

Stein, Bob. "Reading and Writing in the Digital Era." Discovering Digital Dimensions, Computers and Writing Conference, 23 May 2003, Union Club Hotel, West Lafayette, IN. Keynote Address.

# Part 1

Fletcher, Emily. *Stress Less, Accomplish More*. Bluebird, 2019.

Burton, Linda Roszak. "The Neuroscience of Gratitude." *Wharton Healthcare Quarterly*, Jan. 2017, pp. 17-18.

Kini, Prathik, et al. "The Effects of Gratitude Expression on Neural Activity." *NeuroImage*, vol. 128, 2016, pp. 1-10.

Fredrickson, Barbara L. "What Good Are Positive Emotions?." *Review of General Psychology: Journal of the American Psychological Association*, vol. 2, no. 3, 1998, pp. 300-319. doi:10.1037/1089-2680.2.3.300

"Gratitude Is Good Medicine." *UC Davis Health*, 25 Nov. 2015, www.health.ucdavis.edu/medicalcenter/features/2015-2016/11/20151125_gratitude.html.

Orr, Anne, et al. "Living with a Kidney Transplant: A Qualitative Investigation of Quality of Life." *Journal of Health Psychology*, vol. 12, no. 4, July 2007, pp. 653–662, doi:10.1177/1359105307078172.

Csikszentmihalyi, Mihaly. *Flow: The Psychology of Optimal Experience*. New York, Harper & Row, 1990.

Cherry, Kendra. "Why Our Brains Are Hardwired to Focus on the Negative." *Verywell Mind*, 29 Apr. 2020, www.verywellmind.com/negative-bias-4589618.

Kotler, Steven. *The Art of the Impossible: A Peak Performance Primer*. Harper Wave, 2021.

Goodridge, Clare Sarah. "Practice Gratitude to Unlock Your Best Self." *What Is Gratitude?*, Flow Research Collective, 9 Oct. 2020, www.flowresearchcollective.com/blog/practice-gratitude.

Grant, Adam. *Give and Take*. Viking, 2013.

Ackerman, Courtney E. "What Is Self-Transcendence?" *PositivePsychology.com*, 25 Mar. 2022, www.positivepsychology.com/self-transcendence/.

Wood, Alex M., et al. "Gratitude and Well-Being: A Review and Theoretical Integration." *Clinical Psychology Review*, 2010. doi:10.1016/j.cpr.2010.03.005

# Part 2

Robinson, Adam. "New Study Finds 40 Percent of Employees Feel Isolated. Here's How to Make Your Workplace More Inclusive— and Productive." *Inc.com*, Mansueto Ventures, 25 Mar. 2019, www.inc.com/adam-robinson/new-study-finds-40-percent-of-employees-feel-isolated-heres-how-to-make-your-workplace-more-inclusive-and-productive.html.

Steven Huang, Steven. "Why Does Belonging Matter at Work?" *Blog.SHRM.org*, SHRM, 3 July 2020, www.blog.shrm.org/blog/why-does-belonging-matter-at-work.

Brown, Brene. *Braving the Wilderness: The Quest for True Belonging and the Courage to Stand Alone*. Random House, 2017.

Carr, Evan, et al. "The Value of Belonging at Work." *Harvard Business Review*, 16 Dec. 2019, www.hbr.org/2019/12/the-value-of-belonging-at-work.

Locklear, Lauren, et al. "Building a Better Workplace Starts with
Saying 'Thanks.'" *Harvard Business Review*, 26 Nov. 2020,
www.hbr.org/2020/11/building-a-better-workplace-starts-with
-saying-thanks.

Krznaric, Roman. *Empathy: Why it Matters, and How to Get It*. Penguin,
2014.

Hall, Judith, and Mark Leary. "The U.S. Has an Empathy Deficit."
*Scientific American*, Springer Nature, 17 Sept. 2020,
www.scientificamerican.com/article/the-us-has-an-empathy
-deficit/.

The Arbinger Institute. *The Anatomy of Peace: Resolving the Heart of
Conflict*. Berrett-Koehler, 2015.

Smith, Richard, et al. "Envy and Schadenfreude. *Personality and
Social Psychology Bulletin*, vol. 22, no. 2, 1996, pp. 158-168.
doi.org/10.1177/0146167296222005

Emmons, Robert. "Why Gratitude Is Good." *Greater Good Magazine*,
Greater Good Science Center, 16 Nov. 2010,
www.greatergood.berkeley.edu/article/item/why_gratitude_is_
good.

Pratt, Kim, and Elizabeth Hopper. "Mudita: Delight in the Happiness
and Success of Others." *HealthyPsych.com*, HealthyPsych, 6 June
2019, www.healthypsych.com/mudita-delight-in-the-happiness
-and-success-of-others/.

# Part 3

Butman, Joanie. "Price of Suffering." *Choose Wisely*, Choose Wisely,
20 Sept. 2015, www.choose-wisely.net/mediblog/lets-talk/price-of
-suffering.

Doyle, Glennon. *Untamed*. Dial Press, 2020.

Tull, Matthew. "Why People with PTSD Use Emotional Avoidance to Cope." *Verywell Mind*, Dotdash Meredith, 24 Mar. 2020, www.verywellmind.com/ptsd-and-emotional-avoidance-2797640.

Brown, Brene. *Daring Greatly*. Avery, 2012.

Holiday, Ryan. "Coping with Grief: 10 Timeless Strategies from Ancient Philosophy." *The Daily Stoic*, 7 Mar. 2022, www.dailystoic.com/coping-with-grief/.

Manson, Mark. *The Subtle Art of Not Giving a Fuck*. Harper, 2016.

Collier, Lorna. "Growth After Trauma." *Monitor on Psychology*, vol. 47, no. 10, 2016, p. 48. www.apa.org/monitor/2016/11/growth-trauma

Frankl, Victor E. *Man's Search for Meaning*. Beacon Press, 2006.

Gloria, Christian T. and Mary A. Steinhardt. "Relationships Among Positive Emotions, Coping, Resilience and Mental Health." *Stress and Health: Journal of the International Society for the Investigation of Stress*, vol. 32, no. 2, 2016, pp. 145-156. doi.org/10.1002/smi.2589

Tugade, Michele M. and Barbara Fredrickson. "Resilient Individuals Use Positive Emotions to Bounce Back From Negative Emotional Experiences." *Journal of Personality and Social Psychology*, vol. 86, no. 2, 2004, pp. 320-333. doi.org/10.1037/0022-3514.86.2.320

McCullough, Michael E. and Charlotte vanOyen Witvliet. "The Psychology of Forgiveness." *Handbook of Positive Psychology*, edited by C. R. Snyder and Shane J. Lopez, Oxford University Press, 2002, pp. 446-458.

Watkins, Phillip C., et al. "Taking Care of Business? Grateful Procession of Unpleasant Memories." *The Journal of Positive Psychology*, vol. 3, no. 2, 2008, pp. 87-89.

Kashdan, Todd B et al. "Gratitude and Hedonic and Eudaimonic Well-being in Vietnam War Veterans." *Behaviour Research and Therapy* vol. 44, no. 2, 2006, pp. 177-99. doi:10.1016/j.brat.2005.01.005

Riley, Kristen. "Benefit Finding." *Encyclopedia of Behavioral Medicine*, edited by Marc D. Gellman, Springer, Cham, 2020. doi.org/10.1007/978-3-030-39903-0_628

Cassidy, Tony et al. "Benefit Finding in Response to General Life Stress: Measurement and Correlates." *Health Psychology and Behavioral Medicine* vol. 2, no. 1, 2014, pp. 268-282. doi:10.1080/216 42850.2014.889570

McMillen, J. Curtis and Rachel Fisher. "The Perceived Benefit Scales: Measuring Perceived Positive Life Changes After Negative Events." *Social Work Research*, vol. 22, no. 3, 1998, pp. 173-187. doi.org/10.1093/swr/22.3.173

Junger, Sebastian. *Tribe: On Homecoming and Belonging*. Twelve, 2016.

"The Hope That Kills You." *Ted Lasso*, season 1, episode 10, AppleTV, 2 Oct. 2020. *Warner Bros. Entertainment Inc. and Universal Television LLC.*

Van der Kolk, Bessel. *The Body Keeps the Score*. Viking, 2014.

Buckley, Kelly. "Grieving with Gratitude." 2017 Wellness Conference. National Fallen Firefighters Foundation, 7 May 2017, Embassy Suites by Hilton Charleston Historic District, Charleston, SC. Keynote Address.

Ofei, Michael. "What's Your North Star? A Short Guide in Defining Your Purpose." *The Minimalist Vegan*, 18 June 2021, www.theminimalistvegan.com/north-star/.

LaFrance, Adrienne. "An A.I. Says There Are Six Main Kinds of Stories." *The Atlantic*, Atlantic Media Company, 1 Nov. 2018, www.theatlantic.com/technology/archive/2016/07/the-six-main -arcs-in-storytelling-identified-by-a-computer/490733/.

Algoe, Sarah B. "Find, Remind, and Bind." *Social and Personality Psychology Compass*, vol. 6, no. 6, 2012, pp. 455-469. doi.org/10.1111/ j.1751-9004.2012.00439

# Part 4

Fredrickson, Barbara L. "Gratitude, Like Other Positive Emotions, Broadens and Builds." *The Psychology of Gratitude*, Feb 2004, pp. 144-166.

Greenwald, Anthony G. "The Totalitarian Ego: Fabrication and Revision of Personal History." *American Psychologist*, vol. 35, no. 7, 1980, pp. 603-618. doi.org/10.1037/0003-066X.35.7.603

Kumar, Amit and Nicholas Epley. "Undervaluing Gratitude." *Psychological Science*, vol. 29, no. 9, 2018, pp. 1423-1435. doi:10.1177/0956797618772506

Granovetter, Mark S. "The Strength of Weak Ties." *American Journal of Sociology*, vol. 78, no. 6, 1973, pp. 1360-1380.

McPherson, Susan. *The Lost Art of Connecting*. McGraw-Hill Education, 2021.

Uzzi, Brian, and Shannon Dunlap. "How to Build Your Network." *Harvard Business Review*, Harvard Business Publishing, 1 Aug. 2014, www.hbr.org/2005/12/how-to-build-your-network.

Chapman, Gary. *The 5 Love Languages*. Northfield Publishing, 2010.

Burkeman, Oliver. *Four Thousand Weeks: Time Management for Mortals*. Farrar, Straus and Giroux, 2021.

Kibbe, Kayla. "Men, You're Bad at Receiving Gifts. Here's How to Be Better at It." *InsideHook*, InsideHook, 8 Nov. 2021, www.insidehook.com/article/advice/why-men-bad-receiving-gifts.

Haidt, Jonathan. "Wired to Be Inspired." *Greater Good Magazine*, Greater Good Science Center, 1 Mar. 2005, www.greatergood.berkeley.edu/article/item/wired_to_be_inspired.

# Part 5


Schembra, Chris. "How Leaders Can Increase Emotional Intelligence through Open-Ended Questions and Gratitude." *Rolling Stone*, Penske Media, 20 Aug. 2021, www.rollingstone.com/culture -council/articles/leaders-emotional-intelligence-questions -gratitude-1212687/.

Voss, Chris. *Never Split the Difference: Negotiating As If Your Life Depended On It*. Harper Collins, 2016.

Siegel, Kelly. "Council Post: How Cultivating a Culture of Gratitude Can Improve Your Workplace for All." *Forbes*, Forbes Magazine, 12 June 2018, www.forbes.com/sites/forbes humanresourcescouncil/2018/06/12/how-cultivating-a-culture-of- gratitude-can-improve-your-workplace-for-all/?sh=6b8fdaf75226.

Grant, Adam and Francesca Gino. "A Little Thanks Goes a Long Way." *Journal of Personality and Psychology*, vol. 98, no. 6, 2010, pp. 946- 955. doi.org/10.1037/a001793

Elton, Chester. *Leading With Gratitude*. Harper Business, 2020.

McGonigal, Kelly. *The Upside of Stress: Why Stress Is Good for You, and How to Get Good at It*. Avery, 2012.

Coleman, Joey. *Never Lose a Customer Again*. Portfolio, 2018.

McFeely, Shane, and Ben Wigert. "This Fixable Problem Costs U.S. Businesses $1 Trillion." *Gallup.com*, Gallup, 7 Dec. 2021, www.gallup.com/workplace/247391/fixable-problem-costs -businesses-trillion.aspx.

Bureau of Labor Statistics, U.S. Department of Labor. "Hires and Quits Rose in 2017." *The Economics Daily*, 23 March 2018. https://www.bls.gov/opub/ted/2018/hires-and-quits-rose-in-2017.htm

Williams, Lisa A. and David DeSteno. "Pride and Perseverance: The Motivational Role of Pride." *Journal of Personality and Psychology*, vol. 94, no. 6, 2008, pp. 1007-1017. doi.org/10.1037/0022 -3514.94.6.1007

# Part 6

Gladwell, Valerie, et al. "The Great Outdoors: How a Green Exercise Environment Can Benefit All." *Extreme Physiology and Medicine*, vol. 2, no. 3, 2013. doi.org/10.1186/2046-7648-2-3

Lebowitz, Shana. "How the Former CEO of Campbell Soup Used a Skill We All Learned as Children to Inspire Teamwork and Affection in His Company." Business Insider, *Business Insider*, 1 Sept. 2016, www.businessinsider.com/why-leaders-should-show -gratitude-to-their-employees-2016-9.

Toepfer, Steven M. and Kathleen Walker. "Letters of Gratitude: Improving Well-Being through Expressive Writing." *Journal of Writing Research*, vol. 1, no. 3, 2009, pp. 181-198.

Twist, Lynne and Teresa Barker. *The Soul of Money*. W. W. Norton Company, 2003.

Printed in Great Britain
by Amazon